Zen Under the Gun

ZEN
UNDER THE
GUN

FOUR ZEN MASTERS FROM TURBULENT TIMES

Translated and introduced by

J.C. Cleary

WISDOM PUBLICATIONS • BOSTON

Wisdom Publications
199 Elm Street
Somerville MA 02144 USA
www.wisdompubs.org

Library of Congress Cataloging-in-Publication Data
Zen under the gun : four Zen masters from turbulent times / translated and
introduced by J.C. Cleary.
    p. cm.
Includes bibliographical references and index.
ISBN 0-86171-592-6 (pbk. : alk. paper)
1. Zen Buddhism--Doctrines. I. Cleary, J. C. (Jonathan Christopher)
BQ9268.3.Z47 2010
294.3'420427--dc22
                                        2009044738

14 13 12 11 10
5   4   3   2   1

Cover design by Philip Pascuzzo. Interior design by Gopa&Ted2. Set in Book-
man 9.35/16.

Contents

Introduction

A Moment in History

Imagine a world at war generation after generation. A heavily militarized empire reigns supreme, planting its garrisons in country after country, plundering resources, subjugating populations, killing and maiming at will, ruthlessly destroying the cities and towns of anyone who dares to resist.

The empire claims that heaven has given its lords dominion over all the lands and peoples of the earth, the right to rule, the power to decide who survives and who dies. The proof? Their all-conquering armies. What other proof is needed? Might makes right.

In the conquered countries, the people face choices. For the humble people, the farmers and artisans who produce the crops and all things useful, the only hope is that the new rulers will not enslave them and their children, or take the food from their mouths and drive them to ruin. For the well-born people, the educated people, there is the option to retain their privileges by going to work for the conquerors, to sing their praises, to staff their bureaucracies.

The conquerors too suffer distortion. At the top, there is constant intrigue and struggle, as the commanders fight each other for the richest share of the loot. The original warrior bands become more and more hierarchical, as they gorge themselves on the spoils of war, and the war chiefs take the lion's share. Back home the families of the fighters off on distant expeditions are left adrift. If and when the men come back, they return habituated to violence and mayhem.

Does it take much effort for us today to imagine such a world? We too live in a world that has been at war for generations—however often we are invited to forget this, this war over the horizon, this war for our minds. What may be hard for modern people to imagine is how an empire could be imposed without telecommunications, without the tools of industrial technology, without spy satellites and airstrikes and "death from above."

Seven hundred years ago it was the Mongols who achieved this feat, spreading their domain from their remote homeland over Central Asia and China and Russia and Iran and the Middle East. For the Mongol conquerors, armored cavalry was the ultimate weapon, and messengers riding the imperial roads the fastest means of long-distance communication, yet with these simple tools they conquered a wide expanse of Eurasia. Such determination, such tenacity!

The Buddhist teachers whose words are translated in this book were giving lessons to people who lived face to face with tyranny. They had seen the Chinese social order overthrown by outsiders who cared nothing for its values, customs, and cherished patterns of living. All around them people's lives were being snuffed out capriciously and livelihoods being snatched away unfairly. Tyrants rode high, the old notions of justice seemed to vanish.

What was the fate of those who lived through such a catastrophe? Those Chinese whose identities were anchored in the social conventions of a crumbling world went down with it. Opportunists, if they were lucky, found new niches serving the new rulers. Outsiders were brought into China from other parts of the Mongol empire to serve the new masters as officials, merchants, and ritualists. The farmers and artisans could only trust in fate and hope for the best, or flee to the mountains and marshes as outlaws, or take refuge in underground religions promising secret community and millenarian renewal.

The Zen adepts who lived through this era of war and upheaval answered to the imperatives of the bodhisattva path. There was no uniform response. Some continued the teaching by working in obscurity among the common folk. Some worked within the forms of popular religion. Some contributed to the high culture of the elite. Some went into the lion's den to exert a civilizing influence on the warlords.

For the Zen adepts, how to engage in the world was not decided by sentiment or ideology. Part of the repertoire of the enlightened person is to know when and where and with whom to exert effort, and how to be effective. In Buddhist terminology, these are two of the four wisdoms of the enlightened person: *the subtle observing wisdom*, which gives an accurate view of the patterns of cause and effect operating in a situation, and *the wisdom to accomplish works*, which perceives how worthy goals can be achieved in a given environment.

All we can be sure of as outsiders is that the air of serenity we sense in the words of the Zen teachers of the time was not a reflection of the social reality around them. The alleged deeply spiritual nature of traditional Asia is a figment of the modern imagination. In reality the Zen teachers whose words are translated here carried out their work in the midst of a society poisoned by militarism and the clash of mutually hostile cultures.

All through the ages, there have been people who hope to find in Buddhism a way out of the chronic problems and pressures inherent in the everyday world. The more turbulent the times, the more people want to escape into a peaceful realm of contemplative retreat, where they can finally calm down and get comfortable, or at least comfortably numb. This may be why Buddhist teachers through the ages have warned that this escapist approach can be an illusion and a snare.

In the *Lotus Sutra* the Buddha tells his listeners that he taught methods of cultivating detachment as a way to help people progress beyond the madness and futility of self-centered living. But the inner peace and quiet to be gained by this approach, the Buddha explains, is only a temporary resting place, where would-be travelers on the path to enlightenment can stop and rest and muster their strength and courage, until they are fit to continue on way to being bodhisattvas. The real goal of the teaching is to enable people to unlock their potential to be bodhisattvas, that is, enlightened beings with the wisdom and fearlessness to work for the enlightenment of others.

The pattern of the disengaged monastics hiding from the world has been criticized down through the ages as a basic distortion of the Buddhist path. Far from being a creation of Buddhists in the modern West, "engaged Buddhism" has always been an integral part of the true teaching. The life stories of the Zen teachers whose words are translated in this book illustrate this well. Surrounded by a society immersed in militarism and predatory war, they achieved inner peace, but not by fleeing from the world the people around them were trapped in. They embodied the bodhisattva approach to the world: empty but responsive, emotionally detached but actively involved, with the insight to see what really can help, and the courage to attempt it.

Four Zen Teachers

This book presents a selection of Zen lessons from four teachers whose public lives spanned the turbulent period in Chinese history from the last generation of the Song dynasty (overthrown by the Mongols in 1279) to the first generation of Ming dynasty (which drove out the Mongols, and proclaimed its own reign in 1368). These four Zen masters were all eminent public teachers, and their words reflect the state of the art of Zen teaching in their time. Almost nothing is recorded of their personal lives: the emphasis in the written records is on their teachings.

Hengchuan (1222–1289) was almost sixty when the Mongol conquerors took power in southeast China where he lived and taught.

His disciple Gulin (1262–1329) lived to see the Mongol overlords adopting a veneer of Chinese culture for their regime, even making Confucian philosophy the official orthodoxy.

Gulin's student Zhuxian (1292–1348), after working as a Zen teacher in China, spent the last twenty years of his life in Japan, where he lectured on Buddhism at the court of the new Ashikaga shoguns, and taught at various major temples.

Daian (1347–1403) was a spiritual great-grandson of Hengchuan—his teacher's teacher was Hengchuan's disciple. Daian grew up during the millenarian uprisings that broke the Mongol hold on central China, and reached manhood as the new Ming dynasty was establishing its rule over the country.

On the eve of the Mongol conquest, Zen Buddhism in China was flourishing outwardly, in terms of its institutional prosperity and its social prestige. There was a national system of richly endowed, officially sanctioned Zen temples, complete with splendid buildings, wealthy and well-connected patrons, and flocks of monastic followers. Ideas derived from Zen had so influenced Chinese high culture that even the opponents of Buddhism found themselves using Zen phrases and addressing the philosophical perspectives of Buddhism.

But according to its own authoritative teachers in that period, Zen as a vehicle for the teaching of enlightenment was hanging by a thread. The Zen school, which had originated within Chinese Buddhism as a break with formalism, sentimental allegiance, and clerical routine, was now being engulfed by the very same tendencies. Zen styles were being imitated, while the substance was overlooked. Zen methods were being adopted haphazardly, without the expert insight needed to make them work effectively.

Worldly prosperity was never an end in itself for the genuine upholders of the Zen school. At best, the institutional presence and social acceptance of Zen could be a means to further the real aims of Buddhist teaching: to spread awareness of the possibility of enlightenment, to improve moral and ethical standards in society, to provide for the needy and alleviate suffering. At worst, the wealth and prestige of the major Zen temples presented a chronic danger to the real work, by inviting worldly entanglements as ambitious clerics and upper-class patrons struggled for control over the properties of well-endowed temples.

When temple finances became the first priority, many Zen monks found themselves in the business of catering to the magical thinking and superstitious hopes of the laiety. Prosperous temples became havens for people seeking a comfortable refuge from the demands of ordinary society. Ultimately too, in times of political turmoil, the wealth of the large Buddhist institutions made them prime targets for marauding armies.

The Zen masters whose words are translated below witnessed at first hand all these baleful consequences of the institutional "success" of Zen in medieval Chinese society. They watched the Zen communities becoming swamped with false teachers and insincere students. They saw the classic teaching devices devolving into clever clichés and dead routines. They lived through an era of conquests and uprisings, when many Zen temples were plundered and put to the torch. Despite everything, their basic serenity was untouched, and no worldly disasters could shake their deep commitment to keep the Buddhist life of wisdom alive.

History looks different to those in the ranks of the enlightened teachers. They are not wedded to the self-definitions of their own time and place, and political upheavals that upset such self-definitions do not shake them—when necessary, they may sacrifice their lives, but their life of wisdom is not in danger.

The Zen masters were not like the ordinary Chinese intelligentsia for whom the barbarian conquests of China were devastating blows to their worldview and sense of self. They were not like the careerist monks whose lives fell apart when the institutions that sheltered them lost patronage and prestige.

The Zen adepts also had their own perspective on the history of Buddhism itself. They did not see particular formulations of the Buddhist teaching as eternal verities, or particular institutions as essential to the Buddhist mission. They recognized all the forms taken by Buddhism as provisional in nature—necessarily temporary adaptations to the needs of a certain time and place.

These Zen adepts knew that it was inevitable for concepts and methods and institutions that had originally been useful in promoting awareness to be "captured by the world" and drained of their enlightening effect by being made into objects of emotional veneration and blind allegiance. A major duty of the adept teachers, therefore, was to work against this ongoing process of fossilization, and to make a continuously fresh "living adaptation" of the essence of the Buddhist message for their own time and place.

The Zen Message

The enlightened teachers of the Zen school always pointed to a single reality underlying the vast multiplicity of everyday things and events, and identified a potential inherent in all of us for directly perceiving this reality.

This reality is essentially beyond names, but provisionally it was given many names: Mind, Buddha, the body of reality (in Sanskrit, *Dharmakaya Buddha*), the Buddha-Mind, the mind-ground, the Tao, the realm of reality (*dharmadhatu*), Thusness (*tathata*), the supreme truth, the basic essence, reality-nature, the treasury of light, the womb of the buddhas...

Most of us are not in touch with this reality. Instead, we are wrapped up inside a web of false perceptions, an imaginary reality where selfish desires dominate our actions, and we are trapped in a cycle of endless frustration as we strive to get lasting satisfaction from impermanent experiences. Thus the Zen message challenges us at a fundamental level: it challenges the veracity of our perceptions of the world and our perceptions of ourselves.

Our perceptions of the world are constructed on the basis of our upbringing and cultural conditioning. We do not see reality as it is, but rather a projected image of the world as we have been trained to categorize and judge it. We are looking at the world through a kaleidoscope of conditioned ideas, judgments, and habits of mind.

The "self" we imagine to be a stable, independently existing entity is nothing but a loosely knit, often inconsistent collection of routine perceptions and motivations shaped by our cultural and social conditioning. This is the false self that runs our lives. It enmeshes us in its delusions, and screens out any awareness of the underlying unity, the formless truth that permeates all forms.

Where is this underlying reality to be found? It is all around us, as the Zen saying reminds us: "The one solid esoteric body appears in all the dusty realms of sensory experience."

The complete teaching of Buddhism does not advocate escape from the world into some supposed higher, purer realm. The Buddhist effort is to undo our false ideas, and thus liberate our true selves, so that we can experience what is really there in front of us, and reach the level of clarity and equanimity that makes true compassion possible at last. Detachment from the perceptions of the false self opens the way to effective action in the world, which requires true magnanimity, impartiality, and objectivity.

Like the other expressions of Mahayana Buddhism, the Zen school took as its ideal figure the bodhisattva, the enlightened being who works for the enlightenment of others. For the bodhisattva, nirvana is experienced in the midst of the ordinary world of birth-and-death. As a bodhisattva, the Zen adept is "free to come or go," free to enter into the world of delusion when it serves a beneficial purpose, and free to stand aside from it when that is what the dynamics of the situation call for. The bodhisattva is not motivated by a concern to "do good" in some sentimental sense, but by a consciousness of duty and an awareness of real possibilities.

The records of the Zen school show Zen masters acting in all sorts of ways. Some were teachers, some were not. Some lived in obscurity, ignored by the wider world, others were famous and much sought after. Some withdrew from the established Buddhist institutions of their day, some worked within them, some tried to reform them, some had nothing to do with them. Some adepts were eloquent intellectuals, others were taciturn rustics. Some shunned public affairs, others got involved in politics. Some lived in mountain retreats, others worked in cities and towns. Some spoke against venerating the written word, others collected and published Buddhist texts. Some spoke against ritualism, others ran ritual centers.

Included in the ranks of the Zen adepts were monks and nuns, laymen and laywomen, peasants and gentry, hermits and administrators, poets and painters and storytellers, healers, craftsmen, and eccentric wanderers. The common denominator among the Zen adepts was their enlightened insight, not their outward appearance, station in life, or mode of activity.

Similarly, the concepts and practices taught by the Zen teachers to their disciples and followers did not fall into any one simple pattern. They adhered to the basic Buddhist principle of *skill in means*, which dictates that what is taught correspond to the needs and potentials of the people being taught.

In many settings, Zen masters simply taught basic social ethics, urging their listeners to abide by the norms of reciprocity and mutual respect and moral duty fundamental to social life. When called upon to address men in power, Zen masters regularly reminded them to follow the political ideals embodied in the sage kings of the Confucian tradition: concern for the welfare of the common people, devotion to public duty, leadership by moral example, the image of the true king as the architect of a just social order.

Zen teachers sometimes echoed the themes typical of Chinese popular Buddhism. They invoked the popular ideas of reincarnation and karmic rewards and punishments to urge people to value their time and not waste the opportunities presented by being born human. They urged people to engage in the whole range of merit-making activities, from helping widows and orphans, to giving charity to the poor and helpless, to supporting the upkeep of temples, the production of Buddhist statues and paintings, and the printing of Buddhist books. They encouraged people to turn away from worldly frustrations and find solace from their afflictions in protector-figures like the merciful bodhisattva Guanyin or the buddha Amitabha.

In the era this book focuses on, Zen teachers often urged followers to combine the Zen understanding of mind with the practices of Pure Land Buddhism—reciting the name of Amitabha Buddha, visualizing Amitabha Buddha, taking vows to be reborn in the Pure Land.

In the usual Pure Land understanding, Amitabha is a buddha of the distant past who vowed to save all those who sincerely invoke his name by enabling them to be reborn in his Pure Land, where—free of the afflictions of sickness, suffering, old age, and death—they could progress to final enlightenment.

In the Zen understanding of Pure Land, Amitabha is identical with our innate enlightened mind, and the Pure Land is the purity of our inherent buddha-nature. The Zen adepts found that the Pure Land practice of reciting the buddha-name can be a powerful tool for focusing scattered minds and letting people reorient themselves toward a larger reality usually screened off by the preoccupations of their false selves.

In the course of their teaching activities, Zen masters often emphasized the basic lessons of Mahayana Buddhism. They pointed out the artificial, self-contradictory, impermanent nature of the false self and the inventory of perceptual experiences it sustains. They spoke of the classic Mahayana program for moving beyond the false self, via the "six perfections"—generosity, discipline, patience, energetic effort, meditation, and wisdom. They set forth the ideal of the bodhisattva path, of returning from the "great death" (of the false self) back to life in the world of ordinary people and their illusions, to work for universal liberation by whatever means necessary.

Much of the supposedly mysterious quality of Zen utterances disappears when they are contextualized in terms of the classic Mahayana theories of being and consciousness. This is what I have tried to do in the translations in this book, while letting the characteristic style of the Zen school show through vividly. The four Zen teachers translated here artfully challenge their listeners to live the life of wisdom described in the Buddhist scriptures. They remind people that they are already in the presence of the absolute, and that only the self-created barriers of false perception keep them from realizing this.

As one Zen master put it: "The ocean of reality-nature has no shores. Mountains, rivers, and the great earth are waves on this ocean. Sun, moon, and stars are waves on this ocean. It flows into the nostrils of all the buddhas of past, present, and future. If all of you want to emerge from your bubble of delusion and witness this ocean, go slowly and gently reawaken."

Zen teachers emphasize the moment-to-moment quality of delusion, of conditioned perception, of the false self, of "karmic consciousness." It follows then that the work it takes to awaken from this delusion must proceed on a moment-to-moment level, in all situations, "whether walking, standing, sitting, or lying down."

The very design of Zen talk—the flow of images, the shifting between abstract and concrete, metaphorical and direct, absolute and relative—functions to stimulate the listeners' minds to switch levels and change perspectives, to interrupt the continuity of habitual perceptions and thought patterns.

Effective Zen practice by its very nature cannot be formalized, or made into a routine or a rigid system. Zen methods were often likened to medicines, and Zen teachers to skilled physicians who knew how to prescribe the particular "cure" that would be effective for what ails the particular "patient." In times and places where Zen was alive and well, no legitimate teacher ever suggested a simplistic, "one size fits all" approach.

Depending on the current needs of the individual person in question, genuine Zen teachers directed students into a variety of activities, ranging from study of Buddhist scriptures, to various meditation exercises, to taking on responsibilities in the Buddhist community, to dealing with the surrounding society. Real Zen teachers knew how to monitor their students' spiritual progress and change tactics accordingly.

"Enlightenment stories" loom so large in Zen literature that we sometimes forget that these stories only recount the climactic episodes of what was typically a long, arduous process—"sudden enlightenment" after decades of multifaceted work. From the scattering of more detailed records that remain, we see that Zen people progressed along the path over years and decades of comprehensive effort. Those who reached the goal experienced a series of breakthroughs and mystical states that also had to be painstakingly transcended until their final arrival at the totality.

The Zen people whose teachings are translated in this volume were people who had arrived at this totality. Their words and images sail by on the pure wind of freedom, offering us a glimpse into another state of mind, another state of being, inviting us to move onward to reclaim our true birthright.

Textual Sources

The Chinese texts translated in this book are to be found in the *Zoku Zokyo, The Continuation of the Canon,* a collection of Chinese Buddhist texts that was put together at the beginning of the twentieth century by scholars in Japan. This collection contains many of the records of the Zen teachers from the Song, Yuan, and Ming periods. This collection can be accessed online at suttaworld.org.

The Teachings
of Hengchuan

Fundamental Mind

Hengchuan said, "We should just know where our own minds are born. If we know where mind is born, then we will know where mind functions twenty-four hours a day. If we know where it functions twenty-four hours a day, then we know where it has functioned for countless ages.

"This is why all the buddhas came forth: they wanted to awaken us to our fundamental mind. This they considered the ultimate.

"If you can be like this, then all at once you pay back in full [the benevolence of the enlightened teachers of the past]: you don't have to do anything else. If you do other things, these things belong to the plane of contrived action. How could they be enough to repay uncontrived benevolence? 'The rock of ages will wear through someday, but the Lord's benevolence is inexhaustible.'"

---
*

Uncontrived benevolence: The benevolence of the buddhas and bodhisattvas in communicating the teaching of enlightenment is a spontaneous outflow of their enlightened wisdom, not a calculated effort to do good or win merit by helping others.

Start from Where You Are

A monk asked, "What is the phrase specially transmitted outside the verbal teachings?"

Hengchuan said, "It does not fall into mystery and wonderment."

The monk said, "If so, then it directly enters the stage of Tathagata."

Hengchuan said, "But slowly."

The monk asked, "What is the right course of conduct for me?"

Hengchuan said, "Where have you just come from?"

The monk said, "How can I repay the benevolence of ruler, parents, enlightened teachers, good companions, and all forms of being?"

Hengchuan said, "By starting from the road you were just on."

The monk continued, "How is it when a tiger corners you at the brink of a cliff?"

Hengchuan said, "Life seems to be hanging by a thread."

The monk said, "Help! Save me!"

Hengchuan picked up his staff and tossed it down to the monk.

Then Hengchuan said, "All of you little 'Zen masters' must personally come to clear understanding of your own inherent nature. You shouldn't merely face the fire when you feel cold and go into the shade when you feel hot. You shouldn't accept as inherent nature the one moment of unmoving mindfulness when the elements of which the body is composed disperse. You shouldn't accept me opening my mouth and moving my tongue as *it*.

"The ancients said, 'This nature is originally pure, and contains the myriad qualities. There are differences according to whether it follows defiled or pure objects. Thus, all the sages awaken to it, and always use it purely, and thus they achieve the path of enlightenment. Sentient beings are deluded about it, and always use it in a defiled way, and thus they sink and drown in the karmic cycle. The essence of their inherent nature is not two different things."

Then Hengchuan planted the staff upright and gave a shout.

*
***

The phrase specially transmitted outside the verbal teachings: The meaning of Zen.

Tathagata: An epithet of Buddha meaning "one who has come forth from Thusness." The buddhas, the enlightened teachers, are one with reality-as-it-is ("Thusness"); they come forth to communicate this reality to those locked inside shells of mental conditioning.

Hengchuan picked up his staff: The staff symbolizes the teaching function and salvific work of the Zen adepts.

This nature: Buddha-nature, the potential for enlightenment inherent in all sentient beings; also called by many other names: "inherent mind," "the original face"...

Cutting and Smashing

Hengchuan said, "With the sword of wisdom, we cut apart the net of defilement and craving. With the diamond hammer, we smash to pieces the nest of ignorance.

"[Linji's teaching of] 'the true person without position' [has become a cliché,] a dry piece of shit. [Shakyamuni Buddha's phrase] 'the treasury of the correct Dharma-eye' [has become useless,] a broken bowl. Clear-eyed patch-robed monks cannot distinguish them."

*
***

Linji: The great ninth-century Zen adept who was Hengchuan's spiritual ancestor.

Shakyamuni Buddha: The "historical Buddha," Indian sage from the fifth century BCE who founded Buddhism.

A broken bowl: The common fate of all formulations of the teaching of enlightenment, even the most sublime sayings and concepts of the greatest enlightened teachers like Shakyamuni and Linji, was to lose their effectiveness when they were subjected to routinized veneration, and their practical implications ignored.

Patch-robed monks: A term for Zen monks, whose symbol was a patchwork robe.

Breaking Through

Hengchuan said, "The bamboo thicket was dense: once Xiangyan hit the piece of bamboo, he forgot everything he thought he knew. The red peach was sparkling: once Lingyun saw it he cut off all doubt and confusion.

"Up in the tower chanting praises, at the foot of the meditation bench planting vegetables. Head Monk Sheng said, 'A fierce tiger is sitting right in the road.'"

Hengchuan gave a shout and said, "If you don't have the strength to lift up giant tripods, the strength to uproot mountains, then you'll not find it easy to mount the jet black wonder-horse that covers ten thousand miles in an instant."

*────────────────────────────────

Xiangyan and Lingyun: Two Zen adepts whose breakthroughs came after long effort, by seemingly chance encounters with concrete scenes.

Up in the tower, at the foot of the bench: The goal of Zen is to be able to function on "both sides"—in touch with transcendent wisdom, while serving a useful purpose in the mundane world of ordinary people. But this is most difficult, because attachment to the world can block awakening: *A fierce tiger is sitting right in the road.*

The jet-black horse: The experience of enlightenment, breaking through ordinary perceptions and tasting wisdom—an experience which can be intoxicating for those who have not cultivated the sobriety to withstand it.

Light Rays

Hengchuan said, "The light rays from hundreds and thousands of clear mirrors shine on each other, not holding back from every atom of dust in every land. Heaven is high and the earth is thick; the waters are broad and the mountains everlasting. You must try to say a phrase from before your parents were born."

*

Hundreds and thousands of clear mirrors: All enlightened beings are in communication with each other outside time and space, while functioning in the temporal world, *not holding back from every land*.

Say a phrase from before your parents were born: Express your true enlightened identity, which is eternal, unborn, and undying, independent of causal conditions.

How Can We Say Anything?

Hengchuan said, "Intelligence, sharp wits, conceptual consciousness, thinking, and interpreting: these are the root of birth-and-death.

"Guishan asked Yangshan, 'All phenomena are transcendent: how can we say anything?' As Yangshan was about to open his mouth, Guishan gave a shout. Guishan asked this question three times, and every time Yangshan tried to answer he got shouted at. With his head bowed and in tears, Yangshan said, 'Baizhang told me I'd have to meet more people [of the Path] to succeed. Today, I've met one.'"

Hengchuan gave a shout and said, "[What you're doing is] the root of birth-and-death."

*

Guishan, Yangshan, and *Baizhang* were Zen masters of the classical period. Guishan was Yangshan's primary teacher; Baizhang a senior adept.

Hengchuan gave a shout: Perceiving that his listeners were busy trying to figure out the Zen story he'd just told them—a story meant to interrupt this approach.

We Walk Together

Hengchuan said, "Stepping through heaven's gate and smashing it, it's far-reaching, open, and empty. I join hands with you and we walk together.

"If suddenly someone asks, 'What is Buddha?' it's the one who steps through heaven's gate and smashes it."

This Is Nirvana

On the anniversary of Buddha's death, Hengchuan said, "When the mind of the triple world is ended, this is nirvana. The mountain flowers are red as brocade. The valley streams are deep blue as indigo."

* ———————————————————————————————

The mind of the triple world: Our set of attachments to the things we desire, to forms in themselves, and to the formless experience of meditation; our hopes and fears based on our attachments to past, present, and future. When these are removed, the phenomenal world of mountain flowers and valley streams is still there—as the site of enlightenment.

If You Die Here

Hengchuan said, "Once when [Zen master] Dasui was clearing a field by burning it over, he saw a snake [slither out of the grass], so he took his staff and flipped the snake into the fire. He gave a grunt and said, 'This body I do not spare.'

"If you die here, it is like finding a lamp in the darkness. You will be in the world as if in empty space. You will be like the lotus, which is not touched by the water it grows in. When mind is pure and clear, it transcends all that."

*

> *Dasui* was a student of the great Tang dynasty Zen master Guishan, founder of one of the Five Houses of Zen. Some anecdotes about Dasui are related in Case 29 of the *Blue Cliff Record*.
>
> *If you die here*: If your false self perishes under the impact of Dasui's lesson, your buddha-nature will shine forth with its wisdom, and you can live in the world without being entangled by it.

Provisional Names

Hengchuan said, "Before the world was given form, there was no such name as 'buddha,' no such name as 'sentient being.' As soon as the world is reified, then all these names are there. Though all these names exist, they are just provisional, false names, which never had any real meaning. So do not accept them [as absolutes]. There is nothing to be concerned about: Take care!"

At a Gathering on New Year's Eve

At a gathering on New Year's Eve, a monk came forth from the assembly and quoted a Zen saying: "Bodhidharma did not come to China, the Second Patriarch did not go to India."

Hengchuan said, "Then to whom did 'Mr. Zhang' sell his straw sandals?"

The monk let it go at that.

Hengchuan then said, "The First Zen Patriarch said, 'From mind-moment to mind-moment, like wood, like stone.' The Second Zen Patriarch said, 'Inert, oblivious of objects.' The Sixth Zen Patriarch said, 'Without thinking at all of good and evil.'

"These are commonplace sayings [in Zen circles] and a lot of people settle down in the stream of words. But the patriarchs only wanted you to investigate mind.

"This mind has never been born and cannot perish. Unborn and undestroyed, it is like wood, like stone—spontaneously oblivious of objects, without good and evil. Maitreya said, 'Mind is like empty space. Space has no tracks, but nevertheless sun and moon revolve with regularity.'"

Then Hengchuan said, "Right now it's night on the last day of the last month."

* ———————————————————————————————

> *Bodhidharma and the other Zen patriarchs*: According to tradition this adept from South India introduced the Zen teaching into China early in the sixth century CE. Bodhidharma is counted as the First Zen Patriarch. His Chinese disciple Huike (d. 593) is counted as the Second Zen Patriarch. For the story of the Sixth Zen Patriarch Huineng (d. 713), see *The Sutra of Huineng: Grand Master of Zen*, translated by Thomas Cleary.
>
> *Mr. Zhang* represents Taoism, the indigenous Chinese, pre-Buddhist tradition of illumination. *His sandals* represent the practical methods of the teaching.
>
> *A lot of people settle down in the stream of words*: Repeating Zen sayings like classic formulae, without trying to discover their meaning and apply it to their own lives.
>
> *Maitreya*: The future buddha, due to be born on earth in a time to come to revive the teaching of enlightenment.
>
> *The last day of the last month*: It's later than you think—get to work and investigate your inherent mind.

How Many?

Hengchuan said, "We meet without batting an eyelash, you east, me west. Meeting, we want to call to each other, but bloodline to bloodline we cannot speak. All around is the smell of food, sticking to the seamless, flawless one.

"How many can there be [open to reality]? In the nearby city, unlimited numbers."

*

You east, me west: No contact can be made when the students stay inside their shells of conditioned perceptions and block the teacher's approach.

The smell of food represents all attachments to sensory experience; *the seamless, flawless one* is the underlying one reality.

Totally Abandon Everything

Hengchuan said, "When Deshan saw a monk enter the gate, he would immediately take his staff and hit him.

"When Muzhou saw a monk enter the gate, he would immediately say, 'An obvious case—I spare you thirty blows.'

"It wasn't that these Zen masters wanted the monks to become buddhas on level ground: they just demanded that they *totally abandon everything.*

"These days the Zen communities are insipid and thin, without anyone [worthy to continue the tradition]. The reason is that no one is willing to abandon everything.

"What all of you see right before you—where will you put it when you abandon it? What you harbor in your hearts—where will you put it when you abandon it?"

*

Deshan (781–867): Eminent Zen teacher of the Tang period. See case 4 of the *Blue Cliff Record.*

Muzhou (780–877): Zen adept who generally carried on his teachings in secret, and supported himself as an artisan. See case 10 of the *Blue Cliff Record.*

Become buddhas on level ground: Part of enlightened perception is the wisdom to see the inherent equality of all phenomena, and thus escape artificial distinctions.

The Buddha in the Shrine

At the cremation of the monk who had served as keeper of the buddha-shrine, Hengchuan said:

"You came as keeper of the buddha-shrine: did you realize what this means?

"'The buddha in the shrine' is a person who has completely understood things. From between his eyebrows he emits a filament of white light that lights up the skulls of all the sentient beings in the world.

"There's no place to put the torch [to light the pyre for this one]."

* ————————————————————————————

The buddha-shrine: One of the buildings in the temple complex.

The buddha in the shrine stands for the inherent potential for enlightened perception within each of us, our buddha-nature.

A filament of white light: In many sutras, Buddha communicates visions of wider realities by emitting a filament of light from between his eyebrows that illuminates the minds of beings in countless worlds.

Tricks Are Useless

On the anniversary of the death of his teacher, Master Tianmu, Hengchuan said:

"Baling did not have a vegetarian feast to mark the demise of his teacher Yunmen, nor did he answer questions [on the occasion]: he just imparted three turning words.

"Today on the occasion of the anniversary of the death of my late teacher Tianmu, I do not hold a vegetarian feast, nor do I have three turning words. Do all of you understand why?

"When Tianmu was alive, when I was face to face with him, all tricks were useless.

"So it was when he was alive, and so it should be now that he is dead."

*

Baling (tenth century): A Zen teacher noted for his eloquence, he was a successor of the great teacher Yunmen. Baling said that the exercise of philosophical brilliance is like piling up snow in a silver bowl. See cases 13 and 100 of the *Blue Cliff Record*.

Turning words: Zen sayings with multiple layers of meaning.

Independence

Hengchuan said, "Consider the four great elements: earth, water, fire, and air. A moment free of doubt, and earth cannot obstruct you. A moment free of desire, and water cannot drown you. A moment free of anger, and fire cannot burn you. A moment free of joy, and air cannot blow you around.

"If you are like this, then you are an independent person of the Path who relies on nothing. Enlightenment is born from relying on nothing, from independence. If you awaken to relying on nothing, then enlightenment too is without attainment."

Direct Awareness

Hengchuan said, "All phenomena are without the characteristics we project upon them: what meets the eye is physical form. Transcendent wisdom has no interpretive knowing: it is directly aware of objects.

"I show you this abruptly and directly, but if you do not understand, the directness becomes circuitous."

*

The Buddhist adepts observed that ordinarily people do not perceive reality-as-it-is, which is a flux of cause and effect; instead, people project upon reality a system of categories and judgments they have been conditioned to accept as real. Enlightenment entails the ability to move outside of this conditioning and achieve direct awareness of phenomena as they are.

A direct explanation is *circuitous* in effect if it does not lead to direct understanding.

The Lesson of the Flames

At the stove-lighting ceremony, Hengchuan said this:

"Xuefeng said that all the buddhas of past, present, and future are in the flames of the fire, turning the great wheel of the Dharma. Yunmen said that the flames expound the Dharma for all the buddhas of past, present, and future, and all the buddhas of past, present, and future stand there and listen.

"I tell you all: All the buddhas have turned the wheel of the teaching on an intimate level, and the flames have explained the teaching on an intimate level. If you do not want to bring on uninterrupted hellish karma, do not slander the Tathagata's True Dharma Wheel!"

Xuefeng (822–908): Drawn to Buddhism from childhood, he pursued his studies traveling from teacher to teacher for many years, and achieved liberation in his forties. He guided a large community of seekers, and helped many awaken. See cases 5, 22, 49, and 51 of the *Blue Cliff Record.*

Worlds and Lands

A monk asked, "What is the meaning of the ancestral teacher coming from the west?"

Hengchuan said, "Ocean water does not freeze." Then he went on to say:

"The one solid esoteric body appears in all the dusty realms of experience. All the worlds in the ten directions are empty and deserted. All the lands of the galaxy are cold and silent."

* ——

The ancestral teacher coming from the west refers to Bodhidharma bringing the Zen transmission from India to China.

The one solid esoteric body: Absolute reality, which permeates the objective and subjective worlds of all sentient beings.

All the worlds in the ten directions: All the worlds throughout the universe. The Buddhist scriptures regularly spoke of the existence of countless numbers of worlds inhabited by sentient beings, spread across the galaxies.

Empty and deserted, cold and silent: Sentient beings do not really exist apart from the one solid esoteric body—their false personalities and conditioned minds are essentially unreal.

Diamond Eye, True Self

Hengchuan said, "Mountains and rivers and the great earth are all a diamond eye. They are also our true self. Adepts with a mastery of methods join together and witness this. There is no facing toward or facing away from the Great Path. There are no verbal explanations of the Absolute Truth. It goes far beyond the three vehicles and rises high above the ten stages."

* ——

Diamond eye: A basic part of enlightened perception is called the Great Mirror Wisdom, the perception that all phenomena are part of one absolute reality, like images appearing in a mirror. The diamond is a metaphor for indestructible clarity, cutting through illusion.

The three vehicles: The three levels of the Buddhist teaching, as described for example in the *Lotus Sutra*, and often referred to in Zen teaching. These are: the teaching of detachment from self and nirvana beyond the world, directed at literal-minded disciples; the teaching of interdependent origination directed at solitary illuminated ones contemplating cause and effect; and the teaching of the nonduality of wisdom and compassion, being and nonbeing, for bodhisattvas dedicated to working for the enlightenment of all beings.

The ten stages: The stages through which bodhisattvas progress; see *The Flower Ornament Scripture* (Thomas Cleary, translator), book 26.

The Fall of Words

Hengchuan said, "Deshan said, 'There is no birth-and-death to be feared, no nirvana to be gained, no bodhi to be experienced: just an ordinary person without concerns.'

"When Deshan talked like this, a concern was born. With a concern born, how could we not fear birth-and-death? With fear of birth-and-death, there is nirvana to be attained and bodhi to be experienced.

"Brothers, do not make collections of words!"

* ───────────────────────────────────

Bodhi: Sanskrit for "enlightenment."

The Infinite Ocean

Hengchuan held up the staff and said, "The ocean of reality-nature has no shores. Mountains, rivers, and the great earth are waves on this ocean. Sun, moon, and stars are waves on this ocean. It flows into the nostrils of all the buddhas of past, present, and future. If all of you want to emerge [from your bubble of delusion and witness this ocean], go slowly and gently reawaken."

Yes and No

A monk asked Hengchuan what Zhaozhou meant when he said a dog has no buddha-nature.

Hengchuan gave a great laugh.

The monk said, "I do not understand why you laugh."

Hengchuan said, "I'm laughing because you are slow-witted, a bucket of dark ignorance."

The monk went on, "Zhaozhou was also asked, 'All sentient beings have buddha-nature: why not the dog?' Zhaozhou said, 'Because he has karmic consciousness.' Is this really true or not?"

Hengchuan said, "What is there that's not really true about this?"

The monk went on, "Another time Zhaozhou was asked if a dog has buddha-nature, and he said it does. How could he have said both things?"

Hengchuan said, "The Zen elders everywhere are like this."

The monk went on, "When he was asked why we go into this leather bag [of ignorance], Zhaozhou said, 'We knowingly offend.' Please, master, explain this clearly."

Hengchuan said, "[It's as if you're saying] 'Look how many Zen stories I've memorized!'"

Then Hengchuan said, "The Bird's Nest Monk blew on the fuzz of a cloth, and his attendant awakened."

Then he held up his staff and said, "Beyond the sky, the clouds end. In the grass, the snakes are startled."

* ——————————————————————————

The Zen elders everywhere are like this: Answering questions according to the potential of the situation and the listeners, not offering fixed definitions of a truth that is undefinable by nature.

The Bird's Nest Monk gave his attendant the last push he needed to finally awaken after years of effort.

Beyond the sky, the clouds end: Outside the self-created world of deluded perception, nothing can block the sun of reality.

In the grass, the snakes are startled: Within the orbit of deluded perception, Zen teachings astound those who hear them.

The Zen Family Song

Hengchuan taught the assembly:

"*This affair* requires that each person awaken for himself. The
buddhas of past, present, and future have neither transmitted nor
been given the Dharma, nor have the six generations of Zen patriarchs, nor have all the Zen masters in the world.

"A monk asked Linji, 'Whose family song do you sing? Whose
Zen style do you inherit?' Linji said, 'When I was at Huangbo's
place, I asked three times and was beaten three times.' The monk
hesitated, thinking. Linji then shouted and followed up with a
blow, telling him, 'You can't drive nails into empty space.' How can
you drive nails into empty space?

"There was a lecturer-monk who asked Linji, 'Surely the multi-
farious Buddhist scriptures illuminate buddha-nature?' Linji said,
'The wild grasses have never been hoed.' The lecturer said, 'How
could Buddha cheat people?' Linji said, 'Where is Buddha?' The
lecturer was speechless. Linji said, 'If you're trying to deceive me
in front of my constant companions, you had better leave at once.'

"Look at how Linji acted. Was there any transmitting or receiving? Even awakening was absent. It has been like this through
countless ages past, up until today.

"If we compare this with what belongs to each and every one of
you, none of you is lacking in the least. 'Having eaten, wash out
your bowl.' Sometimes we might say something to ourselves,
sometimes we might say something to someone else, but there is
never any false or true.

"Right now I am speaking a phrase: it shatters the polar mountain into atoms of dust and gathers together the four great oceans

into a single pore. In one meaning it creates countless meanings and in countless meanings it creates one meaning.

"[Here are some famous Zen sayings:]

A fragrant wind comes from the south, producing a slight chill in the depths of the palace.

Sentient beings are inverted: they lose themselves and pursue things.

If you can transform things, you are the same as a Tathagata.

For the Tathagata, the one who comes from Thusness, there is no coming and no going. Thus he is called Tathagata.

"For these sayings, you don't have to search. Just observe that the five clusters are all empty and the four great elements have no stable identity, and directly, suddenly comprehend completely.

"In the assembly, you are constantly 'understanding Zen.' So I ask you, what is Zen? It is not a moment of mindfulness empty and illuminated. It is not utter stillness. Study is not it. Awakening is not it.

"[The saying goes:] 'A moth can land anywhere, but it cannot land on the flames of a fire. Sentient beings can become attached to any object, but they cannot become attached to prajna.'

"One brushstroke wipes it out. The workman in the stone room forgot his steps as he walked the treadmill. Where has he gone?"

*

The six generations of Zen patriarchs: According to tradition, the Zen teaching was brought from India to China by Bodhidharma, who was succeeded by Huike (487–593), who was succeeded by Sengcan (d. 606), who was succeeded by Daoxin (580–651), who was succeeded by Hongren (601–674), who was succeeded by Huineng (638–713). These six men are reckoned as the "six patriarchs" of Zen; from them, the Zen schools in China branched off in many directions.

Huangbo (d. 850) was an influential Zen teacher, among whose disciples was Linji, after whom the Linji School of Zen is named. See case 10 of the *Blue Cliff Record*. Huangbo said, "The buddhas and all sentient beings are just one mind, there is nothing else."

You can't drive nails into empty space: You cannot capture the reality of the Path in fixed formulas, procedures, and concepts.

The wild grasses have never been hoed: You speak of the scriptures, but your understanding of them is overgrown with your own subjective interpretations.

Having eaten, wash out your bowl: Having received a nourishing, illuminating teaching, do not cling to it, or make it an object of attachment.

The five clusters: The aggregates which make up the experiential world of sentient beings: form, sensation, perception, volitional synthesis, and consciousness.

The four great elements: Conceived as making up the physical body: earth, water, fire, and air.

Prajna: Transcendent wisdom, a nondualistic awareness that encompasses both absolute and relative, both real and provisional, both the absence of stable identities and the interplay of cause and effect, without imposing categories such as self and others or subject and object.

The workman in the stone room: The Third Patriarch of Zen, Sengcan, who was defrocked during an anti-Buddhist persecution and forced to work as a laborer.

The Mark of True Reality

Hengchuan said, "The physical body is a form. The Dharma-body is reality-nature. All good and evil depend on the Dharma-body, not the physical body.

"Ordinary people only see the physical body; they do not see the Dharma-body. They cannot carry out procedures without fixed forms. They cannot carry out the practice of equanimity in all places. They cannot universally respect all sentient beings.

"Those who see the Dharma-body are able to carry out procedures without fixed forms, and so are able to respect all sentient beings, and thus practice *prajnaparamita*, the perfection of transcendent wisdom. This is the mark of true reality. All of you should detach from the five skandhas and the four elements, and come forward and meet with me."

* ───

> *Prajnaparamita*: Sanskrit for "wisdom going beyond," meaning the wisdom of the enlightened people that enables them to see the one reality underlying all phenomena, to see the inherent equality of all things, to see the real pattern of cause and effect at work in situations, and to accomplish good works within specific environments.
>
> *The five skandhas*: The aggregates which make up the experiential world of sentient beings: form, sensation, perception, volitional synthesis, and consciousness.
>
> *The four elements*: Conceived as making up the physical body: earth, water, fire, and air.

What a Dead Man Sees

At the cremation of a dead monk, Hengchuan said, "Xuansha said, 'In front of the face of a dead monk, what meets the eye is *bodhi*.'"

Hengchuan picked up the torch [to light the pyre] and said, "The fire at the end of the eon sweeps through and the whole universe is destroyed: only *bodhi* is not destroyed."

* ───

> *Xuansha* was a fisherman who became a student and later a colleague of Zen master Xuefeng. See cases 22 and 88 of the *Blue Cliff Record*.
>
> *Bodhi*: Sanskrit for enlightenment.

The Lion's Roar

Hengchuan said, "Even if you overturn the great ocean and kick down Mount Sumeru, even if you scatter the white clouds with your shouts and break apart empty space, you still haven't managed to be half a patch-robed monk. The style of our school is vast and great, awesome in virtue and power, sovereign and independent.

"That's why, at the assembly on Spirit Peak, the broad-browed butcher could throw down his slaughtering knife and say, 'I am one of the thousand buddhas!'

"In the great congregation, demon kings of great power are waiting until all sentient beings become buddhas and their worlds are empty: only then will they generate the mind of enlightenment.

"True lion cubs are good at the lion's roar."

* ————————————————————————————————

> *Mount Sumeru*: In Indian cosmology, the world is pictured as composed of four continents arranged around a colossal polar mountain in the middle—Mount Sumeru. In Zen parlance, Sumeru often stands for the phenomenal world as a whole.

> *The assembly on Spirit Peak*: Where Buddha inaugurated the Zen transmission.

> *The great congregation*: The great congregation of Mahayana Buddhism, which teaches that all sentient beings have buddha-nature, and all share an ultimate common destiny—to become enlightened.

> *The lion's roar*: Symbolizes the experience of awakening to reality.

Poison

Hengchuan went up to the hall and summoned the assembly and said to them, "Form and sound are deadly poison to birthlessness. Sensation and conception are pitfalls for perfected people." Then he left the seat.

*

Birthlessness: The state where the dualistic mind does not arise, where reifying conceptions are not projected on the phenomenal world, and thus where all phenomena are seen essentially fused with the unborn reality.

Witness

In 1272 Hengchuan was invited to be abbot of Nengren Temple at the behest of the leading monks in the capital area. At a small gathering on the night he entered the temple, Hengchuan said:

"How could I have intended to be abbot at this temple? Previously, my becoming enlightened was also unintended. My coming here is due to other people, people acting for the sake of the Buddha Dharma.

"The Buddha Dharma does not belong to me: I have witnessed it, that is all. Still, to witness it is not an easy thing.

"Right now, should I affirm? Should I negate? Should I cut off affirmation and negation both at once?

"This is the mark of reality: above, no clinging with awe; below, no personal self. The eternal light appears, standing like a ten-mile-high wall."

Hengchuan brandished his staff and gave a shout.

Buddha Is Served in All Places

Hengchuan said, "In one world they think Buddha is served with sound. In another world they think Buddha is served with incense and food. If you cling [to any method] and lose proper proportion, you are sure to enter into deviant paths.

"Here at Nengren we think that Buddha is served in all places. All the countless buddhas of the past and future are all right where you are standing. Do you realize that?"

Then Hengchuan said, "A sutra says, 'When body and mind are pure, all phenomena are pure.' A Zen master said, 'When all phenomena are pure, then body and mind are pure.'"

Hengchuan gave a shout and said, "Tell me, which side does this shout fall on?"

Then he said, "In a single shout, host and guest are distinguished: perception and action proceed simultaneously. If you can understand the meaning in this, 'at noon we signal midnight.'"

* ——

Host and guest: The absolute and the relative, Buddha and sentient beings, true reality and conditioned perceptions; in other contexts, the host is the teacher, the representative of reality, and the guest is the student, the inhabitant of delusion.

At noon we signal midnight: From the absolute perspective, delusion does not exist, and so neither does enlightenment—we're "already there." Operating within the world of delusion, it is necessary to make the distinction and talk of being liberated from delusion and entering into enlightenment—we have to work so we can "arrive."

No Sentient Beings Without Buddha-Nature

Hengchuan said, "To go from human to buddha: this is clinging due to holy sentiments. To go from human to hell: this is clinging due to profane sentiments. When sentiments of profane and holy are both purified away, humans *are* buddhas and buddhas *are* humans. To think that there are sentient beings without buddha-nature, or insentient things with buddha-nature—these are false views."

Where Buddha Taught

Hengchuan said, "The places where Buddha taught, such as the Egret Pond and the Vulture Peak, the seashore and the forest groves, are no different from here. Right now, what Dharma am I preaching?

"If your conceptual faculty is still stuck, you simply must come forward and get sorted out. Baofu had a saying: '[Realization arrives like] a spark struck from stone, or a flash of lightning—whether you succeed or not, you won't avoid losing your body and your life.'"

* ———————————————————————————————

Baofu (d. 928) studied with Zen master Xuefeng and later helped many others find the path. See cases 8, 22, 23, and 93 of the *Blue Cliff Record.*

The Spiritual Light

Hengchuan quoted this Zen story:

A monk asked Baizhang, "What is Buddha?"

Baizhang said, "Who?"

The monk said, "Me."

Baizhang said, "Do you know 'me' or not?"

The monk said, "It's obvious."

Baizhang held up the whisk and said, "Do you see?"

The monk said, "I see."

Baizhang kept silent for a long while, then said, "The spiritual light shines alone, far beyond sense-faculties and sense-objects. The essence appears real and eternal, not bound by language. The real nature of mind is undefiled, fundamentally perfect of itself. Just detach from false objects, and it's the buddha of suchness."

Hengchuan commented, "'Me' is 'me'—what's the use of 'Do you know "me" or not'? Before the Zen teacher holds up the whisk, the spiritual light shines alone, far beyond sense-faculties and sense-objects. After he holds up the whisk, the spiritual light shines alone, far beyond sense-faculties and sense-objects.

"[Baizhang said,] 'The essence appears real and eternal, not bound by language. The real nature of mind is undefiled, fundamentally perfect of itself. Just detach from false objects, and it's the buddha of suchness'; but [I say to you that] Mount Sumeru is blocking your throats, and the water of the great ocean is pouring into your nostrils."

*

> *Before the Zen teacher holds up the whisk, the spiritual light shines alone*: The whisk symbolizes the active role of the teacher in pointing out reality, but reality is already there.
>
> *Mount Sumeru is blocking your throats*: Unless you are at Baizhang's level, your attachment to the phenomenal world still obstructs your potential for enlightenment.

Reflections of the Moon

Hengchuan said, "Truly great people have another *living shore*. Their spirits are not confined to themselves, and they do not worship others as sages. To them the six Zen patriarchs in China and the twenty-eight in India were just reflections of the moon in the water, just illusory flowers in the sky."

*

> *The moon* symbolizes the one reality; *the water* stands for the flowing phenomenal world.

Zen History

Hengchuan said, "Born today, dead tomorrow. The Zen school is a thousand-year-old field that has gone through eight hundred owners. Zen today is a broken-down house that no one will repair."

Karmic Consciousness

On New Year's Eve, Hengchuan said, "Karmic consciousness is vague and boundless, without a basis that can be relied on. When you reach the evening of the last day of your life, you will be just like a crab dropped into boiling water.

"The dawn bell has sounded: the colors of daybreak are evenly parting the sky. We join to celebrate the new year, but you are still attached to sense-objects. For eons countless as the sands, you have flowed along wildly through birth-and-death, like water-wheels, never stopping."

A Rock Enclosing Jade

At the cremation of a monk, Hengchuan said, "It's like the earth holding up a mountain, unaware that the mountain is singular and steep. It's like a rock that encloses jade, unaware that the jade is flawless. Pines are straight, brambles are twisted. The straight are used as building materials, the twisted are burned as firewood."

* ────────────────────────────

A comment on the relation of our transient physical bodies and conditioned minds to our buddha-nature.

What Are You Listening With?

Hengchuan said, "Do not bring up the ancients: just discuss right now. All of you are here listening to the Dharma. What are you listening with?

"If you are listening with your ears, ears are a sense-organ: how can you hear the Dharma? If you are listening with your eyes, eyes are a sense-organ: how can you hear the Dharma? If you are listening with your mind, mind is a sense-organ: how can you hear the Dharma? My Dharma is formless: your listening must be formless.

"The great teacher Linji said, 'If you want to be liberated from birth-and-death, from going and staying, and reach freedom, just recognize right now that the one listening to the Dharma is without shape or form, without root or basis, without abiding.'"

Sharing the World's Doubts

Up in the hall a monk came forth and asked, "When Zen master Danxia burned a wooden buddha for warmth, why did the temple director's eyebrows fall?"

Hengchuan said, "This is precisely what I have doubts about."

The monk said, "Master, you are an enlightened teacher. Why do you too have doubts?"

Hengchuan said, "When no one in the world has doubts, then I will have no doubts."

The Pure Light

Hengchuan said, "The purity of mind is Buddha. The light of mind is Dharma. What is not the pure light? Even the mountains and rivers and the great earth, the sun, the moon, and the stars, are all the pure light."

Take a Step Back

Hengchuan said, "What's the benefit of a lot of book-learning? Just take a step back and let the solitary light reflect on itself and awaken to the sensory dusts. To establish nothing at all is still a great fault."

* ————————————————————————————

> *To establish nothing at all is still a great fault*: Because realizing emptiness is not the final destination; the enlightened person must return to the world of the dusts and work for the enlightenment of others.

Clumsy Descendants

Hengchuan said, "Heaven covers everything, earth holds up everything. Sun and moon shine on everything. Bodhidharma came from the west, crossing the flowing sands of the desert. His later-day descendants through trying to play clever have become clumsy."

"In each and every one of us there is a world..."

Hengchuan said, "In each and every one of us there is a world, a world that the earth cannot hold up and that space cannot contain. I'll take mine and throw it down in front of all of you people. Can all of you take yours and throw it down in front of me?"

The Impermanence of Impermanence

Hengchuan said, "Eminent monks, don't just be like sly dogs chasing a false objective. Realize impermanence in your present moment of mind. All worldly things with shape and form are swallowed up by impermanence. Impermanence too is swallowed up by impermanence. If you can awaken to the impermanence of impermanence, this is the true self of all of you."

No Other Move to Make

At a small gathering on New Year's Eve, Hengchuan said, "On Spirit Peak, Shakyamuni Buddha held up a flower, and Kashyapa gave a slight smile of tacit understanding. At Shaolin, Bodhidharma faced a wall, and the Second Patriarch's mind was pacified. In my speech and silence and motion and stillness throughout the year I have no other move to make.

"Even if you are all fundamentally complete and perfect, and you can mesh with the true source when the bell sounds and the magpies cry, how will you tell us about it?"

Who Are You?

One day Hengchuan saw one of the brethren quoting ancient and modern Zen sayings, and asked him, "What connection does this have to your own lot?"

The monk had nothing to say.

Hengchuan hit him with the staff and said, "Are you the one who quotes ancient and modern, or are you the one who cannot open his mouth?"

Win the Race

On midsummer's day up in the hall, Hengchuan quoted Longya's verse:

To study the Path first you must have some enlightenment
    as a means.
It's like racing speedy dragon-boats:
Though afterward you're back in your old place on open
    ground,
Only having won the race can you rest.

Hengchuan picked up his staff, threw it down, and returned to the abbot's quarters.

* ———————————————————————————

Longya (834–920) studied with both Zen Master Dongshan, seen retrospectively as one of the founders of Caodong (Sōtō) Zen, and Zen master Linji, seen as the founder of Linji (Rinzai) Zen. The story of Longya's awakening is told in case 20 of the *Blue Cliff Record.*

The Wheel of Food

At a vegetarian feast for the monks, Hengchuan said, "The wheel of food turns, the wheel of Dharma turns. I join my palms and hold them over my head [in a gesture of supplication]. In the scriptures Buddha says, 'Giving alms to you [unworthy] monks should not be called a field of merit. Those who contribute to support you are falling into the three evil planes [to be reborn in hell, as hungry ghosts, or as animals].'"

* ———————————————————————————

The wheel of food refers to concerns about economic security, social status, and reputation that were the real motivations for many in the Buddhist clergy. *The wheel of Dharma* means the teaching of truth for its own sake.

Don't Wait

At the cremation of the assistant director of the temple, Heng-chuan said:

"Your whole life you were intelligent and intellectually sharp, full of plans and calculations. When you come here [to the funeral pyre], none of this can be used. So better kill off mind and body: don't wait to be straw thrown on the flames."

* ——————————————————————————————————————

> *Kill off mind and body*: Like other wisdom traditions, Buddhism emphasizes "dying before you die," putting an end to the conditioned self and its attachments in order to experience reality-as-such.

Teaching Zen

Hengchuan quoted an ancient Zen saying: "When a strong man flexes his arm, he doesn't depend on anyone else's strength. Someone good at twirling a sword does not cut his hand."

Hengchuan held up the staff and said, "Stretching the body across space and time, setting the guiding principles with a single phrase."

Neither/Nor

Hengchuan said, "If a single thing exists, Vairochana falls among the ordinary mortals, not to return for eternal ages. If the myriad things do not exist, Samantabhadra loses his realm and has no place to go."

* ——————————————————————————————————————

> *Vairochana* Buddha, the cosmic illuminator, represents the absolute reality ceaselessly reaching to sentient beings.

Samantabhadra, the bodhisattva whose name means "Universal Good," represents all the manifestations of the enlightening work being carried on in all forms in all worlds.

Charity

On one occasion when the patrons of the temple were present in the monks' meditation hall, Hengchuan said, "Standing everywhere like a mile-high wall, clear in all particulars, the eternal light appears. In the scriptures it says, 'Morning, noon, and night, using countless bodies to give charity.'"

Tools

Hengchuan cited this Zen meditation case:

> Once when Baizhang went up to the teaching hall, Sheng of Yunyan came forward and asked, "Every day you go into such fine detail: for whom?"
>
> Baizhang said, "There's a person who needs it."
>
> Sheng said, "Why don't you tell him to do it for himself?"
>
> Baizhang said, "He has no tools."

Hengchuan commented, "Where is the person who needs it? Even though he has no tools, it will only work if we make him do it himself."

Turning the Wheel of the Dharma

Hengchuan held up the staff and said, "The staff is on top of all of your heads turning the great wheel of the Dharma. All the buddhas of past, present, and future are underneath your feet, turning the great wheel of the Dharma so that all sentient beings achieve true enlightenment."

Formation, Abiding, Destruction, and Emptiness

At the cremation of Master Yanqing, Hengchuan said, "Formation, abiding, destruction, emptiness [are the phases every world-system goes through, according to Buddhist cosmology]. Formation is the elements temporarily coming together to form one's own body. Abiding is occupying the carved wood bench [acting as teacher]. Destruction is the elements coming apart, so that one's own body no longer exists. Emptiness is when light and dark and form and void are not separated at all."

Hengchuan lifted up the torch [to light the pyre] and said, "The nature of fire is originally empty. Formation, abiding, destruction, and emptiness—they cannot be disassociated from each other. Everything is like this. But when your perception penetrates the root source, you grow flowers on stone."

* ——————————————————————————————

Grow flowers on stone: To bring forth enlightening deeds from the original emptiness, for the sake of saving sentient beings (who themselves are originally empty).

The Lotus in the Mud

Hengchuan said, "The enlightened enter the ordinary world and they enter the holy realm, they enter defilement and they enter purity, they enter reality and they enter the conventional plane. Why so? The lotus flower is born from the swampland mud.

"A verse says:

> The lotus flower is born from the swampland mud:
> The standard is naturally special.
> Before and after it emerges from the water,
> The lotus feeds both fish and turtles."

* ───────────────────────────────────

The lotus flower represents enlightenment; *the swampland mud*, the world of ignorance, craving, and aggression.

Both fish and turtles: Enlightenment nourishes all beings.

Washed in Fire

At the cremation of an administrator-monk, Hengchuan said:

"He spent his time down on the farm, overseeing the production of rice for the community of monks, all covered with dust and grime. Now he returns and jumps into the fire to bathe, and transcends Vairochana's pure body."

* ───────────────────────────────────

Down on the farm: In Hengchuan's time, the large monasteries typically had landed estates with peasant tenants working them; managing these estates was one of the administrative posts sometimes held by senior monks.

"If it's not your own question…"

A monk asked Hengchuan about the divergent answers offered by two Zen masters to a famous koan:

"When someone asked Zhaozhou the meaning of the coming from the west, Zhaozhou said, 'The cypress tree in the garden.' When someone asked Qingyun, he said, 'There is no cypress tree in the garden.' Both were asked the meaning of the coming from the west, so why weren't the answers the same?"

Hengchuan said, "If it's not your own question, Reverend, then I don't know either."

Indestructible

At the cremation of a dead monk, Hengchuan said:

"Each and every one of you has a bit of wondrous, illuminated, true nature. When the fire at the end of the age sweeps through, and the whole world is destroyed, this nature is not destroyed.

"Reading scriptures, sitting in meditation, opening up the robe [to relax], extending the bowl, benefiting people and participating in communal labor, being born and dying, movements and actions —all of this is this reality-nature.

"You don't know where it is just because of a moment of being deluded by falsity, of turning your backs on enlightenment and joining with the dusts. You don't know where it's at, so I have pointed it out for you.

"Retreat! Retreat! A fire-snake is coming to pierce your skulls!"

Then Hengchuan threw down the torch [and lit the pyre].

* _____

Turning your backs on enlightenment and joining with the dusts: Spurning your own inherent potential for nondualistic direct perception, and becoming absorbed instead in attachments to the sensory world.

A *fire-snake* represents the flames of the funeral pyre, hence, the inevitability of death.

Tied and Bound by the Intellect

To the assembly of monks at the temple Hengchuan said:

"All the brethren in the hall come to my quarters to ask me to give public talks, hoping these talks will become popular in the Zen communities.

"But this affair is not a matter of words. All his life, Bimo just held up a forked stick. All his life, Judi just raised one finger. All his life, Master Dadi just beat the ground. Even if Zen masters like these split open Mount Taihua and shattered the Yellow River [with their direct teaching methods], they would still not be able to receive one or a half [sincere students]. If I could speak so that heavenly flowers showered down, that would be even more useless.

"Each and every one of you in this great congregation has the potential to become a realized human being—[to reach the stage where,] twenty-four hours a day, there is not the least defilement; where, in the heaps of red dust, you are lifted with the waves; where, in the reflections of the green mountain, you are blown higher and higher. This is the moment when [as in the sutra] the butcher throws down his slaughtering knife and becomes a buddha then and there.

"Just don't form intellectual understandings like this. If you do, you fall into intellectualism, and are tied and bound by your intellects. You are rolled along chaotically and cannot take a step [in wisdom]. You are obstructed by light when it is light and by darkness when it is dark. With form you are obstructed by form; with emptiness you are obstructed by emptiness; with words you are obstructed by words. This is why you fall into birth-and-death, the sea of suffering, with no capability of emerging.

"As for the ancients, where they stood was solid reality, so naturally they were crystal clear on all sides. They could pick up a dead snake and make it come alive. Haven't you read this story?

"A monk asked Mazu, 'What is the meaning of the patriarch coming from the west?' Mazu called him nearer. When the monk approached, Mazu hit him and said, 'Not even three people have the same opinion [about this].' Master Nan of Huanglong said, 'The ancients even said that three people do not agree, so how could three or five hundred? Extensive discussions are a disaster, a disaster.'

"How can intellectual knowledge figure this out? You can go on figuring until Maitreya comes down to be born, but there is no way for you to find out anything. You must forget intellectual knowledge and put an end to all your maneuvers and tricks. It's like seeing the myriad images in a clear mirror with nothing concealed at all.

"When you are not obstructed anywhere, when you can designate a deer as a horse and make south into north, when you let go or gather in with freedom in every move, only then can you come forth to extend a hand as a Zen teacher without blinding the students' eyes.

"For years now the Zen community has been a wilderness, a deserted ruin. The main reason is that those occupying the teacher's seats have been intellectualists. They say that this public case is helpful to people and that one is not. They are happy when people raise the issue alone and play with it: they think this is transcendent grasp. They are afraid when people speak of mind or reality-nature: they think that these are the principles of Buddhism.

"There is also another type of false teacher. They specialize in creating new and strange sayings, and think that this is going beyond convention. They try to influence those who have newly entered the congregation.

"If our school had been like this, how could it have reached the present day? Take a look at Deshan and Linji, at Zhaozhou and Muzhou and Yunmen and all the other elders. What standard did they set? They have a face: it comes to you—do you see? Is there anywhere for you to approach? Since ancient times, they have shone forth like sun and moon.

"The Sixth Patriarch told the assembly, 'I have something with no head and no tail, no name and no word, no back and no front. Do all of you recognize it?'

"Then Shenhui of Heze came forward and said, 'It's the fundamental source of all the buddhas, which is my own buddha-nature.' The Sixth Patriarch hit him with the staff and said, 'What a talkative monk! It was even inaccurate for me to call it "something"—how much the more so to call it "the fundamental source of all the buddhas"! In the future, even if he puts a thatch roof over his head, this lad will just become a follower of the school of intellectual understanding.' Fayan said, 'When the ancients gave predictions, they were never wrong.'

"Those today who take intellectual understanding as the Zen school are comparable to Heze. If you study Zen without the kind of eye and brains [that Deshan, Linji, and the other classic masters had], you are staying in Buddha's house and eating Buddha's food in vain. You are not as good as a farmer in a village of three families who plants the fields.

"Brothers, turn back to yourselves: right where you're standing, silently focus your mind [on reality]. If you have this kind of eye and brain, then you have seen through the pain of birth and old age and sickness and death. But even then I won't let you go yet. In this gate of ours, it's like the ocean: the farther in you go, the deeper it gets. To succeed, you simply must get to the bottom of it.

"But how can you get to the bottom? [Buddha said,] 'Just have a mind that accepts [the Truth]—you won't be deceived.' Take care of yourselves!"

---

*

> *Bimo, Judi,* and *Dadi* are figures cited as exemplars who worked in obscurity among the people and taught by direct gesture. There are no definite biographical details for them.
>
> *Pick up a dead snake and make it come alive*: Citing a familiar story or concept and bringing out the hidden depths of meaning to help the learner advance.
>
> *Fayan* (885–958) went traveling to learn Zen after studying Buddhism and Confucianism. He became an influential teacher in his time, and wrote a famous work criticizing the decadent tendencies of institutionalized Zen.

Ordinary or Holy?

At a vegetarian feast Hengchuan said:

"To offer people food is good-hearted. To offer people the Dharma is also good-hearted. For three pennies, you get a blackened old crone for a wife. Her hair is not combed, her face is not washed: who knows if she is ordinary or holy?"

Then he gave a shout.

---

*

> *A blackened old crone for a wife*: The bodhisattva is married to the world of birth-and-death, with all its deformities, by vows to work for the enlightenment of all beings, but experiences nirvana in its midst—*is it ordinary or holy?*

The Living Phrase

Hengchuan said, "There is a certain saying. When it is mentioned to people, they all gather in their attention and listen carefully.

This is the saying: 'What was your original face before your parents were born?'

"The ancients did not call this a meditation saying, or else it would have become a dead phrase. Therefore, we do not study the dead phrase, we just study the living phrase. If we meet a dead snake on the road, we stop beating it to death. We bring back the bottomless basket full."

* ———————————————————————————————————

> *The dead phrase* is the formula minus the enlightening effect, the fixed definition, the wise saying learned by rote.
>
> *The living phrase* interacts with the learners' minds and transforms them.
>
> *The dead snake* refers to the false self after its demise.
>
> *The bottomless basket* is the true self.

Cesspool

Hengchuan said, "A little cesspool, a big cesspool—to those who emerge without having been drowned, I have a koan for you: 'What is Buddha?' 'A dry piece of shit.'"

Bag

At the beginning of the summer retreat, Hengchuan said, "You and I, buddhas and ordinary beings, sentient and insentient: we are all things inside a bag. Who would you have tie up the mouth of the bag?"

Nirvana in All Things

Hengchuan said, "Since the beginning, all phenomena have always spontaneously had the characteristics of nirvana. Spring grass is green, summer foliage is dense, autumn winds murmur, winter snowflakes fall."

He held up the staff and said, "From morning till night all of you people are always running up and down."

*

Characteristics of nirvana: The true nature of all things is empty and still, like nirvana.

A Call to Duty

In 1283 the General Controller of Buddhism sent an emissary monk from Yanjing (modern Beijing), the Yuan dynasty capital, to deliver an official summons to Hengchuan, who was then serving at Nengren Temple on Mount Yingdang in Wenzhou, inviting him to become abbot of Guangli Zen Temple on King Ashoka Mountain in Mingzhou.

The previous abbot recommended Hengchuan in glowing terms as a worthy successor of the great Zen teachers Linji, Yangqi, and Ying'an, saying:

"He expounds the Dharma without embellishment, without 'carving and embroidery.' He enters into contemporary expressions and uses them as the diamond king's jewel mortar to pulverize the mountain of aberrant and deluded views.

"Yanjing and Yingdang are far apart, yet the General Controller so honors Hengchuan's path that he has issued a proclamation and sent an emissary with a generous invitation to him.

"Though Hengchuan dwells in retirement in his old age, and it is not the time for him to respond to beings, he will surely be mindful that the Way of the ancestral teachers is going to ruin, and will come to serve as the pillar time-tested by the pressure of the current in midstream."

Yangqi (992–1049) was seen as the founder of the line of Zen teachers to which Hengchuan, Gulin, Zhuxian, and Daian belonged.

Ying'an (1103–1163) was a noted Zen teacher of the Song period who studied with Huqiu, the successor of Yuanwu, author of the *Blue Cliff Record.*

The diamond king's jewel mortar: The enlightened teacher's techniques for counteracting misinterpretations of the teaching.

Answering the Call

Five months later, Hengchuan entered Guangli Temple to take up his post.

When he sat in the teacher's seat, a monk came forward from the assembly intending to ask a question, but Hengchuan held him back with his hand and said, "Stop for now, honored monk, and listen to my disposition of the case."

Then Hengchuan said, "The Buddha Dharma is manifest throughout all the worlds of the ten directions. But within these worlds there are those who are deluded by sense-faculties and sense-objects. Therefore the great teacher Bodhidharma said, 'I originally came to this land to explain the Dharma and to save deluded sentient beings. The one flower will open into five petals and naturally set fruit.'

"When this is brought up, you should suddenly awaken. Then your eyes see form without being obstructed by form and your ears hear sound without being obstructed by sound. All the senses are free from obstructions. Then the imperial wind forms a single expanse and the sun of wisdom is forever secure and bright."

＊ ───

> *The one flower will open into five petals and naturally set fruit*: This saying foretells the division of Zen into the classic "Five Houses" of Linji, Caodong, Yunmen, Gui-Yang, and Fayan.

How Can You Reach It?

Hengchuan said, "Honored monks, if you reach inherent mind, if you fully comprehend inherent mind, then you dwell in pure lands without rejoicing and you dwell in evil worlds without aversion. But how can you reach it, how can you fully comprehend? Where there is birth, there is death. Birth-and-death continues without a stop, so how can you get full comprehension? You must work on this more carefully."

Foxes and Lions

Hengchuan said, "Eyes looking at the clouds, standing like a wall miles high. Head covered with ashes, face full of dirt, slogging through muddy water. The wild fox barks, the lion roars—the lion roars, the wild fox barks. Thirty years later, somebody awakens."

＊ ───

> *Standing like a wall*, the enlightened teacher witnesses the transcendent; *slogging through muddy water*, the enlightened teacher engages with the ordinary world of delusion.
>
> *The wild fox barks*: The conditioned minds of those who hear the teaching spin out useless intellectual interpretations.
>
> *The lion roars*: The enlightened teachers communicate enlightenment.

What's Necessary

Hengchuan said, "There are differences between ordinary people and sages, but their real nature is no different.

"When the weather is hot ordinary people say it is hot: sages cannot say that it's not hot. When the weather is cold ordinary people say it is cold: sages cannot say that it's not cold. It's like this all around the world and all over heaven.

"All that's necessary is to see reality-nature. Once you see reality-nature and become a buddha, then buddhas are ordinary people and ordinary people are buddhas."

You Are Standing on the Ground of Reality

In a talk to the assembly, Hengchuan said:

"In our school, we have nothing, no teaching, no method, to give to people. Bodhidharma's coming from the west was just to bear witness, that's all. Each and every person is inherently complete.

"Coming down through countless ages to today, turning and twisting and looking up and looking down, responding to potentials, receiving beings, shitting and pissing, going in and out of birth-and-death, there has never been the slightest lack or surplus.

"When he met Bodhidharma the great teacher Huike just bowed three times and stood where he was: later he succeeded to the station of patriarch.

"These days if people say so-and-so has Zen or has the Tao, some people take their knapsacks and bowls and run off seeking in all directions. Sentiments are born and their supposed knowledge separates them from reality. Their thinking changes them and their essential being deviates from inherent reality. They go on to bump into the kind of false teachers who point to the east as the west, and this adds more to their upside-down deluded thinking.

"Just put to rest the mentality of frantic seeking, and the fundamental realm will spontaneously appear. How can you put it to rest? If you want to put it to rest, you will not be able to put it to rest. Twenty-four hours a day, whether you are walking, standing, sitting, or lying down—this is where you put it to rest.

"It's like Yajnadatta: looking into the wrong side of a mirror, he wrongly thought he had lost his head, and frantically went searching for it. Where the seeking mind is put to rest, there are no concerns. A buddha is a person without concerns.

"In the old days when I was traveling on foot, I too believed there was such a thing as Zen. For three days and nights I kept my attention on the word *No*, observing it horizontally and vertically, but I could not see through it. My chest felt like a lump of hot iron, but there was no understanding.

"Then I came to the assembly of my late teacher. One day I entered his private room, and he brought up the koan: 'On South Mountain, bamboo shoots; on the Eastern Sea, black marauders.'

"As soon as I tried to open my mouth, he hit me: at that moment I emptied through, and the word *No* was smashed to pieces. How could there be any buddhas? How could there be a self? How could the myriad things exist? This is the fundamental realm, the stage of peace and happiness without concerns.

"Once when a traveling monk came to the place where he stayed, the master of Yushan asked him how to study Zen. The monk said, 'Just contemplate this koan: "On top of a hundred-foot pole, how do you take a step forward?"'

"The master of Yushan believed in this monk, and the monk devoted himself to contemplating this saying. Later, while the monk was riding a mule across a bridge, suddenly he was thrown off. As he got up he said:

>I have a bright jewel,
>Long locked up within sensory afflictions.

Now the sensory dusts are gone and the light is born

Shining on the mountains and rivers and myriad blossoms.

"This realization flowed out from his breast to cover heaven and earth: he did not attain it from anyone else.

"Later on, Yangqi asked [his student] Baiyun, 'Your original teacher [the master of Yushan] had an enlightenment verse: please recite it for me.'

"After Baiyun quoted it, Yangqi laughed.

"Baiyun asked, 'What's wrong with it that makes you laugh, master?' Yangqi said, 'Have you ever seen an exorcism to expel plague? Your teacher wanted people to laugh, but you are afraid when people laugh.' At this, Baiyun had an insight.

"We won't discuss Yangqi's laugh—when Baiyun had insight from this, what truth did he find?

"Brothers, right under your feet, you are standing on the ground of reality. When the mysteries and marvels of the Buddha Dharma have been purified away, you use it freely wherever you pick it up. In the boiling cauldrons, among the embers of the furnaces, on the mountain of swords, among the trees with blades for leaves, you turn the great wheel of the Dharma, and all sentient beings achieve true enlightenment.

"If there is the slightest bit where your perceptual ground is not liberated, then everything that faces you is something that obstructs your breast.

"You can be sure of this: *This matter* does not lie in words. There is not the least bit of bestowing or receiving. There is no way for you to figure it out. There is no place for you to draw up next to it. You simply must generate a brave and bold will. Take what you've been keeping wrapped up inside you for half your days, and totally overturn it. Then spontaneously in every move there will be a road to come out on."

*

Yajnadatta figures in a story in the Shurangama Sutra: He looks in the mirror, and thinks the head he sees there belongs to someone else. Imagining that he has lost his own head, he runs into the street screaming, looking for his head. Your buddha-nature is there, you just can't see it in the mirror of your false self.

The word No: Many Zen practitioners in this period made the word *No* their meditation point, or koan. A monk asked Zhaozhou: "Does a dog have buddha-nature or not?" Zhaozhou said: "No."

On top of a hundred foot pole: Total concentration on emptiness.

Boiling cauldrons, etc. represent the afflictions of the hells sentient beings inhabit.

This matter: The business of realizing enlightenment, bringing your buddha-nature into action in the everyday world.

A road to come out on: A way to manifest your enlightened nature.

Cutting Through

Hengchuan said, "The early buddhas had the ability to emanate rays communicating enlightenment across diverse worlds. The ancestral Zen masters had *the Last Word* as the final impenetrable barrier. Both were brought forth in front of people to smash the nest of clichés of interpretive knowledge, and to cut off birth-and-death root and branch.

"[If you do this], then the true essence appears alone, and the wondrous function is wholly real. In a single atom of dust you reveal the land of the Jewel King, and inside a pore you turn the great Dharma Wheel."

*

The Last Word: The word that expresses the reality that cannot be expressed in words.

The essence is the one reality that permeates all things. *The function* is the enlightening work of the buddhas and bodhisattvas.

The Jewel King: Dharmakaya Buddha, the absolute reality.

Illusory Transformations

Hengchuan said, "Once forms and images are born, sorrow and joy immediately follow. Once forms and images are extinct, how could there be sorrow and joy? You must observe birth and extinction: this is the basic source of all the buddhas and it is the illusory transformation experienced by sentient beings."

Hengchuan picked up the staff and said, "Light and dark, form and void—all are illusory transformations."

A Tiger Bit a Tiger

Hengchuan said, "How can you turn the physical world back to yourself? How can you turn yourself back to the physical world? Last night on the mountain, a tiger bit a tiger."

Bring the Cat

Hengchuan said, "The sound of the drums bites apart your monk's robe, so just put on a plain shirt. Rats are running around all over the ground: bring the cat!"

Real Giving

At a vegetarian feast to which he had been invited by Zhang Chaofeng, a powerful patron of Buddhist institutions, Hengchuan said:

"All the worlds in the ten directions are the precious light of the relics of Shakyamuni Buddha. All the worlds in the ten directions are the patrons of King Ashoka Temple.

"Our lord Zhang Chaofeng possesses great wisdom and great perception: before it is raised, he already knows, and before it is mentioned, he already understands. Thus he has come here to the mountain with incense and flowers and candles and tea and fruit and precious things to offer to the Buddha, the Dharma, and the Sangha.

"The assembly here before our eyes is the Sangha. What is the Dharma? The five thousand forty-eight volumes of the scriptures. What is the Buddha? Pure non-doing. This one great marvel is inconceivable, and the benefit to be gained by it is no small matter either. The merit is like the water of the deep blue sea, and endures as long as Mount Taihua. Its children and grandchildren make it manifest and propagate it: the precious treasury is full."

Then Hengchuan planted the staff upright and said, "I only hope that the spring wind will apply its power evenly and year after year blow in through our gate."

He also spoke a verse:

When the one making the offering
And the one receiving the offering
Are both without abiding or attachment,
This achieves *dana paramita*, the perfection of giving.

The Buddha, the Dharma, and the Sangha: The "Three Jewels" of Buddhism, to which Buddhists traditionally dedicate themselves: the enlightened one, the teaching of enlightenment, and the community of practitioners, sometimes conceived narrowly as the monks and nuns, sometimes more broadly as the community of all seekers.

The five thousand forty-eight volumes of the scriptures: A conventional figure to represent the vast scale of the Buddhist canon.

Dana paramita, the perfection of giving or generosity, the first of the six perfections cultivated in Mahayana Buddhism, requires that the giver give without any attitude of gaining merit or selfish advantage, and without taking any self-satisfaction in giving charity.

Right Before Your Eyes

Hengchuan said, "Before your eyes there are no phenomena [as such]: your ideation is before your eyes. It is not phenomena [as you perceive them] before your eyes, [but the absolute reality]. This cannot be reached by ears and eyes. We climb up the green vines, straight up to the top of the cold pine, where the white clouds are flavorless and pure, appearing and disappearing in the great void."

* ───────────────────────────────────────

> *The green vines* represent the living teachings; *the cold pine* is reality itself; *the white clouds* are transient phenomena—if we are not attached to them, they in themselves are pure and do not block enlightenment.

Liberation Right Where You Are

Hengchuan said, "With liberation right where you are, you get great security and stability. Extending the bowl, you eat food. Opening your robe, you open an eye. You are on the summit of a solitary peak, yet you are still at the crossroads. You are at the crossroads, yet you are still on the summit of a solitary peak."

* ───────────────────────────────────────

> *The solitary peak* represents absorption in the absolute.
>
> *The crossroads* represents engagement in the ordinary world.

Mirror Wisdom

Hengchuan said, "Shake the dust from your eyes and reflect together [with all the enlightened ones] on the unbiased mirror.

"When a foreigner comes, a foreigner appears in the mirror.

"When a native comes, a native appears in the mirror.

"When neither a foreigner nor a native comes, what then?
"Profoundly clear."

* ───

> The mind of an enlightened person is likened to a mirror that impar-
> tially reflects all that appears before it without being moved by any
> of it.

The Great Work

Hengchuan said, "Transcend the ordinary and enter into sagehood
here and now, so that you are not confused by the many delusive
demons—this is called 'already completing the great work.' If the
iron wheel is turning on the top of your head, you will never lose
the perfect illumination of concentration and wisdom."

The Mind-Seal

Hengchuan said, "The mind-seal of subtly wondrous illumination.
Seal the Buddha with it—then one hand points to heaven, one
hand points to earth. Seal the Dharma with it—then the dog car-
ries the imperial amnesty in his mouth, and all the grandees step
out of the way. Seal the Sangha with it—then everyone's bowl
opens toward the sky.

"Are there any here who seal themselves with it? If you seal
yourself with it, then whether walking, standing, sitting, or lying
down, you clearly understand every particular.

"At the assembly on Spirit Peak, Buddha transmitted this mind-
seal. On Few Houses Peak, Bodhidharma transmitted this mind-
seal."

*

One hand points to heaven, one hand points to earth: According to the traditional account, this was the gesture Shakyamuni Buddha made when he was first enlightened.

The dog represents the purified personality now empowered by the truth; *the grandees* represent the worldly entanglements that have lost their power.

Bowls open to the sky: Able to receive sustenance from the realm of reality, the cosmos as a whole.

Few Houses Peak: According to tradition, the place in North China where Bodhidharma settled, and where his disciple Huike encountered him.

A Eulogy for Bodhidharma

On the anniversary of Bodhidharma's death, Hengchuan held up incense and said:

"He did not engender aversion when he beheld evil. He did not offer praise when he observed good. He did not abandon the wise and approach the ignorant. He did not spurn the deluded and go to the enlightened. Comprehending the Great Path, mastering the Buddha Mind, he went beyond all measures. He did not share the same routines with the ordinary or the holy. He was transcendent, so we call him our ancestral teacher, our patriarch."

Then Hengchuan took the incense and hit the brazier three times. He asked the assembly, "Do you understand? Pure wisdom wondrous and complete, its essential body inherently empty and still."

Finding Without Seeking

Hengchuan said, "Not a single thing comes out from inside, not a single thing enters from outside. Without cutting off birth-and-death, ending birth-and-death. Without seeking nirvana, arriving at nirvana."

Fire

At the stove lighting ceremony, a monk came forward and asked, "The fire god comes looking for fire."

Hengchuan said, "He returns with green leafy firewood to burn."

Then Hengchuan said, "When the ancient mirror is ten feet wide, the stove is ten feet wide. The flames of fire expound the Dharma for all the buddhas of past, present, and future, who all stand there listening. All of you people sit there on the long benches listening."

*
 ───

The fire god comes looking for fire: People inherently endowed with buddha-nature seek outside themselves for enlightenment.

Green leafy firewood: The raw, unregenerate personality, unsuitable as fuel to kindle the fire of illumination.

When the ancient mirror is ten feet wide: Your perception of reality expands with the breadth of your awakening.

Tossing a Ball

Hengchuan quoted Linji: "The Buddha is the purity of mind, the Dharma is the light of mind, the Path is unobstructed pure light everywhere."

Hengchuan commented, "Tossing a ball on a swift-flowing stream."

Let It Burn

At the cremation of the monk who had served as keeper of the canon, Hengchuan said:

"You suffer pain when you are born, when you grow old, when you get sick, and when you die. If you never escape from these four kinds of pain, a broken-down house is not fit to live in—let the prairie fire burn it down."

* ———————————————————————————

A *broken-down house*: Bodily existence when dominated by sentimental attachments and worldly entanglements.

Recognize Yours

When a lady donor was visiting the temple storehouse, Hengchuan said:

"A strong and solid storehouse—every person has one, filled with precious things, but these are not gold and silver. Today, grandmother, you must recognize yours, so that in the future you won't have to ask anyone else."

The Inner Heart

Hengchuan said, "Hundreds and thousands of gates to the Dharma all return to one's inner heart. Wondrous qualities countless as the sands are all within the mind-source.

"Have all of you eaten yet or not? If you've eaten, go wash out your bowl.

"Each of you must personally investigate the Dharma that has no enlightenment, the Dharma that has no delusion, the Dharma that has no neither-enlightenment-nor-delusion. Take care!"

*

Have you eaten? Have you partaken of the resources of the mind-source? If so, do not become attached to its wonders—*wash your bowl.*

Shine Through

At the cremation of one of the temple's workers, Hengchuan said:

"Let out the fire-light of your own samadhi, let it shine through the dark road of eons of birth-and-death. [As the Sixth Patriarch said,] 'Fundamentally bodhi has no tree, and the clear mirror is not the stand.'"

*

Samadhi: stable meditative concentration.

The Sixth Patriarch's saying points out that our real identity, our buddha-nature, is not dependent on our conditioned mind and physical body.

Another Year Begins

At a small gathering on New Year's Eve, Hengchuan said:

"Tonight is the moment in time when the year ends. Everyone has gathered together for an hour of warmth and conviviality. The popular proverb calls this 'keeping the year.'

"It has never been the case that I want to make arrangements for the Buddha Dharma: indeed, the Buddha Dharma cannot be arranged for.

"Touzi said, 'People may change and appear in thousands of types, but they all bring their own burdens.'"

After a long silence, Hengchuan said, "Next year will have another new one. The disturbing spring wind has never ceased."

* ————————————————————————

> *Touzi* (845–914) studied Huayan Buddhism and then Zen, and became an influential Zen teacher. See cases 41, 79, 80, and 91 of the *Blue Cliff Record*.
>
> *The spring wind*: The message of the Buddhist teaching, bringing news of our potential for enlightenment which can bring us to a new life.

Emptiness and Things

Hengchuan said, "The ancients said that all realms are fundamentally inherently empty and still. How can the towering peaks of the mountain ranges and the flowing streams of the rivers and the dense array of myriad images be empty and still?

"Those who are obstructed by things are not few. Those who are obstructed by emptiness are also not few. Emptiness and things are not two, not one. You must understand for yourself: [direct] understanding without [interpretive] understanding is called true understanding."

Is This You?

At the cremation of a monk named Qian, Hengchuan said:

"Falling into all the snares of doubt, being tied down by being and nothingness and other categories—is this you, monk Qian?

"Breaking through all the snares of doubt, escaping from the bonds of being and nothingness and other categories—is this you, monk Qian?

"It's like fire-light: when burning bright and when extinguished, it does not have two natures."

Once You Fall

At the cremation of the monk who had served as the temple's duty distributor, Hengchuan said:

"Once you fall and cannot be helped up, you lose the pure ripe work you have done your whole life, and none is left.

"Right now ten ancient buddhas are in the flames of the fire explaining the Dharma for you: listen well!"

Burned to Ashes

At the cremation of the manager of the temple's wealth, Hengchuan said:

"The skull is smashed, the knowledge obliterated: thirty-six counting sticks are flung into the fire, and burned to a pile of ashes."

* ——————————————————————————————

> The counting sticks symbolize not only the manager's accounting career, but a life within the confines of conditioned judgments and attachments.

The Road of Nirvana

On the anniversary of Buddha's nirvana, Hengchuan said:

"The sun is warm and the wind is mild, here in the second month of spring. The peach blossoms are red and the plum blossoms are white, all over the mountain forests. On the road of nirvana, there is no coming or going: it's one single pure body with no contrived action."

The Golden Spark

At the cremation of the temple's duty distributor, Hengchuan said:

"When you break through the barrier of birth-and-death and see into the basic source of movement and stillness and speech and silence, this is the moment in time when the bottom explodes out of the bucket.

"Nevertheless, studying the Path is like using a fire-drill to make fire. When you get smoke, don't stop there. Keep on going until the golden spark appears. [Later when the fire is blazing] you can warm your feet and warm your head."

* ——————————————————————————

The bottom of the bucket: Ignorance is likened to a bucket full of black sticky lacquer.

You can warm your feet: Wisdom can sustain you.

Gluttony

Hengchuan said, "The whole body is food, the whole body is drink. How many drink themselves to death? How many eat themselves to death?"

Hengchuan held up the staff and said, "Go back to the meditation hall."

Living in Peace

At a small gathering at the start of the summer retreat, Hengchuan said:

"The method of dwelling in peace has already been explained: we just have to practice it faithfully. As we raise and lower our feet, we naturally do not harm living beings. To protect life requires killing the false self; only when this is completely slain can one live in peace. This method too must be practiced faithfully."

Your True Self

At a small gathering at the end of the summer retreat, Hengchuan said:

"The World-Honored One appeared in the world out of compassion. He established long-term and short-term patterns of practice. This summer has been a short-term effort, ninety days. Eighty-nine days have already passed: one day still remains.

"Whether or not you have had some realization, all of you people should not spurn the World-Honored One, and should not spurn your true selves. Your true self is not the one that is a bubble of illusion. It is not the one that is luminous and aware.

"Run everywhere to the centers of the Buddhist teaching, from Mount Tiantai in the south to Mount Wutai in the north. Find out for yourself [what the true self is]."

* ———————————————————————————

The World-Honored One: Shakyamuni Buddha.

Who Is It?

At the stove lighting ceremony, Hengchuan said:

"The tathagatas of past, present, and future speak the wondrous truth. In the flames of the inferno, snow-fire flies. What's in front of us is all listening to the Dharma. Recognize the one right there: who is it?"

* ———————————————————————————

The tathagatas: The enlightened ones, "those who have come from Thusness."

Express Yourself

Hengchuan said, "On the tips of the hundred grasses, divulging the workings of heaven. In the noisy marketplace, revealing true wisdom. Old Shakyamuni Buddha had no place to hide his body— this we'll put aside for now. But how will all of you people say a phrase to express what's under your patched robes?"

*

> *On the tips of the hundred grasses, in the noisy marketplace*: Enlightened beings do their work in the midst of the ordinary world of delusion and social convention.
>
> *Buddha had no place to hide* because his insight had to be expressed to the world; wisdom and compassion are inherently linked.

The Buddhas Never Got Their Way

Hengchuan said, "The buddhas never got their way. The ancestral teachers never got their way. Today I do not get my way. All of you have never gotten your way."

A Snowflake Flies into the Flames

At the cremation of the manager of the temple wealth, Hengchuan said:

"I must show you the fundamental spiritual light. You have come three times as manager of the temple wealth. Sentiments and sense-objects were thick around you. A snowflake flies into the flames of a red-hot furnace."

*

> *You have come three times as manager of the temple wealth*: Hengchuan implies that this man has been stuck at a certain level of aspiration, lifetime after lifetime.
>
> The false self at death is like a *snowflake flying into a red-hot furnace*.

No Tricks

Hengchuan said, "In front of a real person, tricks are totally useless."

*

> A *real person* is one who has activated his buddha-nature and gained enlightened insight into the world of cause and effect and its inhabitants.

Once Attained, Forever Attained

Hengchuan said, "Eminent monks, when you experience the intent of the buddhas, it is unconcerned peace and bliss. Once attained, it is attained forever. It is not the same as Sudhana gathering in his mind for a short while so that the gate of the tower would open to him."

*

> In the climactic book of the *Flower Ornament Scripture*, the seeker-after-truth *Sudhana* is shown marvelous realms of enlightenment inside Maitreya's tower.

Round and Full

Hengchuan said, "Reality-nature is not dirty or clean: it is profoundly clear, round, and full. For the buddhas, it is bodhi; for sentient beings, it is affliction."

Mindfulness

Hengchuan said, "Light and dark, form and void, have never obstructed anyone. One moment of mindfulness permeates countless worlds, and the myriad kinds of daily activities are mastered. Profoundly clear, forever still, always setting your own family style in motion."

The Intimate Secret Is Within You

Hengchuan said, "When monk Ming awakened, what had the Sixth Patriarch just said to him? He had asked, 'Without thinking of good or evil, at just such a time, what is your true face?'

"If I follow this and say the same thing today, why don't all of you awaken?

"Monk Ming bowed to the Sixth Patriarch and asked, 'Besides these intimate words and intimate meaning just now, do you have any other intimate message for me or not?'

"The Sixth Patriarch said, 'If I tell you, it is not intimate. If you reflect back on your own original face, what's intimate is within you.'

"Here the Sixth Patriarch put a cangue on his head and chains on his feet."

* ———————————————————————————

In old China the *cangue* was an instrument of punishment: a heavy wooden frame that was locked around the neck of the person being punished.

The Real You

Hengchuan said, "Eminent monks, fundamentally there is no such thing: you yourselves create doubts for yourselves. Where do these doubts arise? If you recognize where they arise, then and there they are emptied out. All the buddhas of past, present, and future are you. The six generations of Zen patriarchs are you. But you—who are you?"

* ——————————————————————————————————————

> *All the buddhas of past, present, and future are you:* All the enlightened ones of all times and places share the same essence—and this is also the buddha-nature latent in all of us.

Moving Minds

Hengchuan raised the staff and said, "Seeing the temple-flag blowing in the wind, two monks began to argue. One monk said, 'It's the wind that's moving.' One monk said, 'It's the flag that's moving.'

"The Sixth Patriarch told them, 'It's not the wind that's moving and it's not the flag that's moving. Rather, it is your minds that are moving.'

"These two monks and the patriarch have already passed through where all of you are standing now."

Have You Met the Teacher?

A posthumous letter arrived from Master Jue-an. Up in the hall Hengchuan said:

"The elements combined to form his illusory body. With an illusory body, he extricated students from their illusions. The elements separated: how could the illusory body still exist?

"Is there anyone here who has met Master Jue-an right at that moment?"

Let Us Rebuild

When he was about to retire from the abbacy at Guangli Temple, Hengchuan went up to the hall and said:

"Even before we came out of our mothers' wombs, for each and every one of us, our karmic connections [to the Buddha Dharma] were already undeviating.

"I have been dwelling here at this temple for six years now. I hope to rely on the experienced elders and the brethren from all over the country to join together to smash the clichés of the present time, and call back the old sayings from two or three hundred years ago.

"Let it be known that the school of Linji exists, and has never been cut off. From the heap of rubble, let us rebuild a pure sanctuary.

"Today I am retiring with deep contentment in my poor breast. Take care, everyone."

Taking Shape from the Formless

Hengchuan quoted the verse of the prehistoric Buddha Vipashyin:

> Physical existence takes birth from the formless,
> Like the shapes and images produced by a magical illusion.
> The consciousness of the illusory people is fundamentally
>   nonexistent.
> Wrongdoing and merit are both empty, with no place to stay.

Hengchuan held up his staff and said, "The staff [with which Zen teachers teach] also takes birth from the formless."

The Body of Buddha

Hengchuan quoted the verse of the prehistoric Buddha Krakuc-
chananda:

> Seeing that the body has no real substance is the body
>   of buddha.
> Understanding that mind is like an illusion is the illusion
>   of buddha.
> If one can comprehend that body and mind are fundamen-
>   tally by nature empty,
> This person is no different from the buddhas.

Hengchuan commented, "The body of buddha is not solid and
it's not empty. The illusion of buddha is not illusion."

The Esoteric Body

Hengchuan quoted a sutra: "There's just one, solid, esoteric
body—all sense-objects appear within it."

Then he said, "It's you—from morning till night, running up and
down."

He held up his staff and said, "A stinking bag of skin."

Where to Look

Hengchuan quoted Zen master Jiashan: "Comprehend me on the
tips of the hundred grasses, and recognize the sons of heaven in
the noisy marketplace."

Hengchuan commented, "See the ancient buddhas on the end of
the staff."

Emptiness and Form

Hengchuan quoted Zen master Yunmen: "True emptiness does not destroy being. True emptiness does not differ from form."

Hengchuan said, "The green, green thickets of bamboo—all true Thusness. The thick lush yellow flowers—none are not prajna. All sounds are the sounds of buddha, all forms are the forms of buddha. Sentient beings are without defilement."

* ──

In Buddhism, *emptiness* means that phenomena do not have a fixed, independent identity—they are the result of a temporary combination of causal factors, and do not exist in themselves apart from this. Therefore "form is emptiness and emptiness is form." The apparent world is a manifestation of the one reality, the truth-body of a buddha.

The Teachings
of Gulin

Gazing Out Over Infinity

Gulin cited a verse by Master Xuedou:

> Spring mountains in layers of chaotic greens
> Spring waters gushing empty blues
> Vast and vacant between heaven and earth
> Standing alone gazing out over infinity

Is the Path Far Off?

Gulin said, "Is the Path far off? In touch with things, it is real. Is sagehood far away? Embody it and you are spiritually energized. How dense the yellow flowers! We cannot but call them prajna, transcendent wisdom. How green the groves of bamboo! We cannot but call them dharmakaya, the buddha's body of reality.

"Therefore, in reality, on the level of absolute truth, not a single atom of dust is accepted, but in the gate of myriad practices, not a single dharma is abandoned.

"It's fine if all of you believe this and it's fine if you do not. Thirty years from now, when you encounter genuine people of the Path, do not tell them that here at White Cloud Temple my teaching style was like a steep rocky peak and you were never able to get a grip on it."

*

> At the absolute truth level, no phenomenon exists as an independent entity, so *not an atom of dust is accepted.* In practice, the teachers of enlightenment make provisional use of all sorts of methods and circumstances, so *not a single dharma is abandoned.*

Sudden Enlightenment

Up in the hall Gulin said, "The ancestral teachers have told us that the mind-ground contains all the various seeds. Under the universal rain, they all sprout. With the flower called sudden enlightenment, sentiments are over. It's forever alive yet unborn.

"In the thirty-three heavens, among the twenty-eight constellations, in the five thousand forty-eight volumes of the scriptures, among the principles and practices and effects of the teaching, is there such a truth as this?

"The lamp gets up and dances. The pillar raises its eyebrows. Two diamond spirits burst out laughing. A pair of red apricots turn into plums."

*

> To the enlightened eye, even the inanimate world expresses the truths conveyed in the Buddhist teaching. After enlightenment, the world is as it was, but the way it looks to the beholder is transformed.

Useless

Gulin said, "Intellectual comprehension is like a pearl in a bowl. It rolls around by itself even without being pushed. When it comes to comprehending the human lot, it is totally useless."

* ───

> *The bowl* that contains *the pearl* can stand for the conditioning and habits that limit the intellect to familiar ruts.

The Gate of Liberation Is Wide Open

Up in the teaching hall, Gulin spoke a verse:

> The golden wind fans the plain.
> The jade dew bestows its pearls.
> Leaves fall in the forest.
> The hum of the locusts fills the fields.
> The gate to liberation is wide open.
> The real truth extends continuously through the ten
>   directions.
> Everyone's eyes see it, everyone's ears hear it.
> Each and every one goes beyond present and past.
> The one road upward to transcendence
> Has another spot that's difficult to comprehend:
> Its hammer splits you in half
> Above all, do not grasp at it.
> If you grasp at it, that's not like it.
> It strips you of your tongue.
> It stands like a wall ten thousand fathoms high—inscrutable.
> It takes special iron to be beaten into swords.

Real Riches

Gulin cited a Zen saying: "[Buddha's successor] Kashyapa's soiled robe of rags is worth millions. The jewel in the topknot of the king of the world isn't worth half a cent."

Gulin commented, "When the ancients spoke like this, it may truly be said that their benevolence was so great it is impossible to repay."

The Living Intent

Gulin quoted a saying by Master Dongshan: "If there are words in the words, these are called dead phrases. If there is wordlessness in the words, these are called living phrases."

Gulin said, "What are living phrases, you Zen worthies? When we get here, it is hard to find people who know.

"There's another saying: 'You must study the living phrase. Do not study dead phrases. If you comprehend at the living phrase, you will be fit to be a teacher of humans and celestial beings. If you comprehend at the dead phrase, then you will not even be able to save yourself.'

"The great teacher Linji said, 'Here with us is the living intent of the ancestral teachers.' Thus, when Linji asked Huangbo three times about the true great meaning of the Buddha Dharma, he got hit three times: it was like being brushed by a fragrant branch. If Linji hadn't studied the living phrase, how could he have been as he was? The ancients were this way, but modern people are not.

"The living aspect will not let itself be pinned down and cannot be called back. The ancient sages did not make static arrangements: up till now they've never had a fixed location anywhere. Comprehend it on the tips of the hundred grasses!

The old monk in the noisy marketplace
Recognizes his true self.
The spiritual source is bright and clear:
The branching streams flow on in secret."

Uncontrived Action

On the morning of New Year's Day Gulin went up to the hall and said, "All the worthy sages used uncontrived action and thus had differentiating wisdom."

Gulin held up the staff and said, "This is the staff. What is uncontrived action?"

After a long silence he said, "When the mirror is clear, the Path is there. When you try to understand the teaching [with the conditioned intellect], the Path is absent. In space, a stone mortar; in water, a buoyant reed."

* ─────────────────────────────────────

Uncontrived action: Action not motivated by selfish considerations or guided by dualistic perception, action that springs from enlightened wisdom and compassion.

Differentiating wisdom: To accomplish their enlightening work, the buddhas and bodhisattvas need to be able to distinguish true patterns of cause and effect and intervene strategically within them.

When the mirror is clear: When the mind is not obstructed by conditioning and false ideas of self and others, reality is evident.

In space, a stone mortar; in water, a buoyant reed: Wisdom takes action amid emptiness, as a solid tool for preparing medicines; wisdom brings detachment amid passions, floating above them.

Buddha

On Buddha's birthday Gulin said, "Buddha appeared in the world for One Great Cause [to enable sentient beings to open up their inherent enlightened perception]. Mountains and rivers and the whole earth made a great lion's roar [of triumphant enlightenment] and expounded great transcendent wisdom."

Then he held up his staff and said, "Look! Look! Buddha is going into the Deer Park again [to give his elementary teachings]."

What's to Stop Us?

Up in the hall Gulin said, "Not being opposite anything—that is the samadhi of noncontention. The myriad forms cannot hide it: what's to stop us from walking alone through the vastness? Sitting on the tiger's head, gathering in the tiger's tail, without interaction, without taking on a task." After a long silence, Gulin said, "After all tonight's moon is nowhere not pure light."

* ───────────────────────────────

> *The tiger's head, the tiger's tail:* Reality in its formless transcendent aspect and in its phenomenal worldly aspect—the enlightened people master both.

This Gate

At the end of the summer retreat, Gulin went up to the hall and said, "[Our retreat has lasted] from the fifteenth day of the fourth month [mid-June] to the fifteenth day of the seventh month [mid-September]. Let us count off on our fingers: exactly ninety days."

Suddenly he held up the staff and said, "It pierces old Shakyamuni's nostrils. All the tathagatas of the past already perfected this Gate. All the bodhisattvas of the present are entering into its perfect illumination right now. All those people who practice and study in the future will have to rely on this Dharma. Fundamentally it is ready-made of itself. There's nowhere it cannot be: east, west, south, and north, the intermediate directions, the zenith and nadir, up and down, and back and forth in all directions.

"Good people, it was like this when we started the summer retreat, and it is also like this as we end the summer retreat. Preserve and hold this Dharma well for yourselves. For the best people, one decisive break, and everything is comprehended. For the middling and lower sorts, the more they hear the more they don't believe."

Then Gulin planted the staff upright.

Advice to the Monarch

At the conclusion of the ceremony of viewing the Buddhist scriptures at the imperial court, Gulin said:

"It is not made of words. Arrangements of words are not it. The whole great treasury of teachings is all right before our eyes. The body of reality of all the buddhas is perpetually manifest."

"So it's best to take the boundless body of emptiness as the correct body and the indestructible diamond mountain as the mountain of long life.

"How grand the emperor will be, radiating the virtue of the ancient sage kings into all regions of the realm! What sweeping power, as he sends out the imperial wind to the far ends of the empire! The aged and the helpless young, the orphaned and the weak among the people, all get the benefit of his prosperous and just political order.

"The emperor is well supplied with classic examples, and wholly renews cultural practices. The sun of the ancient sage kings shines side by side with the sun of Buddha. The monarch's wheel of gold turns along with the wheel of the Dharma."

*

> *The ancient sage kings* in Confucian lore embodied the virtues of ideal monarchs: they were selflessly impartial, magnanimous and far-seeing, and won the voluntary allegiance of the people by faithfully serving their best interests and working to create a just social order. When face to face with political rulers, Zen teachers in China regularly exhorted them to uphold the Confucian virtues as well as extend their protection to Buddhism.

In Short

Gulin said, "Once the mind's eye is assimilated to reality, one look and we immediately see. Citing a profusion of wise sayings ancient and modern actually shows a lack of skill in means. A single hand does not make a lot of noise [clapping]. A single thread does not make a stringed instrument. When we hold up a single hair, the lion's whole body appears." Then he left the teacher's seat.

*

> *A single hair, the whole body:* To the discerning eye, the truth as a whole is present in each partial truth.

Reaching the Source

Gulin said, "Passed along from buddha to buddha, a boundless land, where self and other are not separated in the least. It's transmitted from enlightened teacher to enlightened teacher, in all times ancient and modern, from beginning to end never departing from the present moment of mindfulness.

"As for the one path upward that the thousand sages do not

transmit, even if you cut off the enjoyment of enlightenment as bliss and the embodiment of enlightenment as compassionate action, you won't avoid falling into the heaps of sound and form.

"If you go further, and on the Other Side of the Primordial Buddha, before the Empty Eon, you energize the mystic wind alone, and illuminate the true self only, this is much like scratching an itch from outside the boot. What liveliness will there be?

"Therefore it is said:

> The single source of all spiritual awareness, of all sentient
>   beings,
> Is provisionally named 'Buddha.'
> Its bodily form disappears but it is not annihilated;
> Its golden streams spread out—still genuine—and always
>   remain.
> The common people use it every day without being aware of it.
> All the buddhas know it forever and use it alone.
> By means of their will to use it alone with no private biases,
> They always dwell prior to what has form.
> With the mind that uses it daily without being aware of it,
> They go far beyond the absolute truth [and enter the relative].
> No before, no after, no ancient, no modern.
> Others and self are mingled in sameness;
> Sage and ordinary are not different.

* ───

The one path upward that the thousand sages do not transmit: Because each person must experience it directly for herself.

On the Other Side of the Primordial Buddha, before the Empty Eon: Names for the ground of being, the state of undifferentiated oneness.

Like scratching an itch from outside the boot: Still separated by a barrier, still not the most intimate level. Here Gulin expounds Zen at its steepest, challenging his listeners to go beyond the ultimate absolute—in terms of meditative experience, beyond utter emptiness, beyond neither-consciousness-nor-not-consciousness—and reach the level of fusion of the absolute and the relative described in the verse.

The Teacher's Staff

Gulin held up his staff and said, "Right now old Shakyamuni is here on the end of my staff, emitting a great light and expounding great transcendent wisdom.

"If there is one word or one phrase in this that does not extract the nails and pull out the wedges and dissolve the sticking points and remove the bonds for all of you, I vow not to achieve true enlightenment.

"Even so, I have only said one half of it. What is the other half?"

He planted his staff upright and said, "Heaven and earth are wide open."

* ———————————————————————————————

> *One half, the other half:* From the perspective of the relative truth, sentient beings are deluded and need to be liberated, to have the wedges pulled out and the sticking points removed. From the perspective of the absolute truth, nothing separates sentient beings from the Source, the one reality provisionally called "Buddha": *Heaven and earth are wide open.*

Buddha Is not Remote

When he was invited up to the teacher's seat by the donors for the Ten Thousand Buddhas Festival, Gulin said:

"Buddha is not remote from humans. Buddhahood is experienced in the heart.

"Where did I get this news? Reality has no attachments: these are born based on sense objects.

"But do not settle down here [beyond attachment]. For people who are quick and lively, as soon as they hear [buddhahood] mentioned, they are like giant golden birds who part the ocean's waters with their wing beats to catch and swallow dragons; they are like lions strolling along who do not seek companions. For them every atom of dust is Thus, every moment of thought is Thus. The whole body comes like this, the whole body abides like this."

The Whole World Is My Patron

Speaking to the patrons of the temple at the festival, Gulin said, "Nanquan said: 'The whole world is my patron.' He wasn't fooling you!"

* ───────────────────────────────

> *Nanquan* (747–834), one of the greatest Zen teachers, studied Buddhist philosophy and the Buddhist scriptures in depth, and finally was enlightened with the help of the great master Mazu. See cases 28 and 31 in the *Blue Cliff Record.*

When the Time Comes

Gulin said, "When the particular time arrives, the truth is spontaneously apparent. The sunlight does not wait for a fire to be warm. The moonlight does not wait for the breeze to be cool. The world is one rod wide, the ancient mirror is one rod wide, the stove is one rod wide.

"Where the buddha-image is big there is much mud. Where the boats ride high the tide is in."

* ───────────────────────────────

> *The world, the ancient mirror, the stove:* Inner and outer align and fuse.
>
> *The buddha-image is big, the boats ride high:* The inflow of truth brings empowerment.

Here and Now

Gulin said, "Today is the start of the new year. Yesterday was the end of the old year. One year and then another year—we just follow along with them like this. Just get so that your body and mind are peaceful and happy, then you will not go wrong with the Buddha Dharma.

"For those who leave home, nothing is not peaceful and happy. Their everyday activities, drinking and eating and turning around and looking down and looking up: aren't these fields of peace and happiness?

> The duck quacks, the sparrow chirps,
> But they can mesh with the true source.
> The wind moves and dusts fly,
> But all illuminate the business of the buddhas."

Gulin took his staff and hit the incense stand and said, "All the buddhas of past, present, and future are here. If you affirm them, the naga girl suddenly becomes enlightened. If you deny them, the star that signals awakening tumbles down."

* ───

> *The naga girl suddenly becomes enlightened*: In the *Lotus Sutra*, to refute an eminent monk who supposes that women cannot become enlightened, the Buddha shows a young girl achieving enlightenment. The nagas in classical Indian lore were the spirits of the oceans.
>
> *The star that signals awakening*: In the story of Shakyamuni's enlightenment, he awakens upon seeing the morning star.

Whose Realm Is This?

Up in the teaching hall, Gulin said, "A thousand waves rising side by side is the family style of Manjushri. A single expanse of clear emptiness is the meditation seat of Samantabhadra. The wind is mild and the sunshine warm, the willows are green and the flowers red—whose realm is this?"

He held up his staff and said, "The fact is that all of you people are putting on the red dusts and entering into the village hamlets. On your shoulders you carry the sun and the moon, on your backs you bear Mount Sumeru. Thirty years from now, do not do people wrong."

Then he held his staff upright and left the teacher's seat.

* ———————————————————————————

> *Manjushri* is the bodhisattva who represents transcendent wisdom. His *family style* is the way of acting of those who live the life of wisdom.
>
> *Samantabhadra* is the bodhisattva who represents the work of universal enlightenment.
>
> *The red dusts*: Sensory experience colored by emotional attachments.
>
> *The village hamlets*: The world of delusion.
>
> *Do not do people wrong* by pretending to teach without having the enlightened insight a teacher must have.

Levels of Meaning

After a ceremony at which the sutras were displayed and chanted, Gulin said:

"In the scriptures it says, 'The Dharma Treasury of verbal teachings in the eighty-four thousand volumes expounded by the Tathagata—these are all called texts, verbal teachings. Detached from all words and sounds and texts and written characters, what theory cannot explain, is called truth.'

"It also says, 'In the scriptures, the written phrases are vast and deep, and make the minds and intellects of sentient beings leap up with excitement: this is called the incomplete meaning, the provisional meaning. [The aspect of the scriptures] that is able to communicate so that mind and intellect become like ashes: this is called the final meaning, the complete meaning.'

"Good people, [I tell you that] if [the so-called incomplete meaning] makes the mind and intellect of sentient beings leap up, then they ought to be able to detach from false entanglements. Having detached from false entanglements, they can merge with the buddha of suchness. So why should this be called the meaning that is not final? If [on the other hand, through the so-called final meaning,] mind and intellect are like ashes, then ultimately, what has been finally comprehended?

"Here on White Cloud Mountain in a period of seven days we have been through the scriptures of the great canon. At each and every word and phrase in its five thousand forty-eight scrolls, we have not thought in terms of words and phrases, and we have not thought in terms of texts and explanations. We have not thought of it as buddha and we have not thought of it as not-buddha. We have not thought in terms of the incomplete meaning or the final meaning.

"What I have just said can be an unlimited cause for good. It is respectfully dedicated to extending the sagely life span of the emperor and the myriad forms of peace."

Our Breath Comes Out in Rainbows

As he was entering Kaiyuan Temple in Pingjiang-fu, Gulin pointed to the temple-gate and said, "Entering the gate, I see the name-plate. Mounting the horse, I see the road. Great Function appears before me as I walk alone through the crimson clouds."

He held up the official document from the Mongol regional authorities [appointing him to be abbot at the temple] and said, "In India they gave the bequest: here in the eastern lands it has been communicated. Hiding sun and moon within our breasts, our breath comes out in rainbows. Where verbal explanations do not reach, the pure wind for a million miles."

He pointed to the teacher's seat and said, "Above we do not see all the buddhas, below we do not see sentient beings, in the middle we do not see ourselves: only then can we ascend to this seat. The thousand-year tree without a shadow—today's bottomless boots."

Then Gulin ascended to the seat. After obeisance was made to the throne, Master Wanchou struck the gavel and announced, "Eminent guests of the Dharma assembly, behold the supreme truth!"

Then Gulin said, "How will you behold the supreme absolute truth? An ancient said, 'It is shining bright between the mind and the eye, but it cannot be glimpsed by giving it form. It is clear as can be in the colored dusts, but reason cannot discern it.'

"Since it cannot be glimpsed or discerned, it follows that eyes, ears, nose, tongue, body, and intellect, as well as [the correlated sense objects] form, sound, smell, taste, feel, and conceptualized things, are all shadow phenomena that have no connection to the supreme truth.

"If you can directly take up the supreme truth, then my stint of work here today as the new elder opening up the teaching hall is done. If not, then if you have doubts, please ask questions."

At the time there was a monk who said, "[I want to ask] about the ancient's saying: 'Knock it down and it's nothing else. Vertically and horizontally [in all directions] it is not sense-objects. Mountains, rivers, and the great earth reveal as a whole the body of the Dharma King.' What does this mean?"

Gulin said, "It penetrates from top to bottom."

The monk continued, "There are no more mountains to block off the colors of the fields. The light of the sky joins directly with the water."

Gulin said, "If you want to fathom the eye that sees a thousand miles, come up another level."

The monk bowed in homage.

*

The thousand-year tree without a shadow—today's bottomless boots: The age-old teaching of truth, majestic, uncanny, contrasted with the broken-down condition of the Zen world of the time.

Eat Your Fill

At the vegetarian feast at the end of winter, Gulin said:

"It is equal in food. It is equal in the Dharma. As it is said, 'This reality is everywhere equal, there is no high or low.' It cannot not be equal in abstruse Zen sayings. Gold is tested with a touchstone, jade is tested with fire."

Then he held the staff upright and said, "I have heard that once you've eaten your fill, you forget being hungry a hundred times. My physical existence today is a case of this." Then he got down from the seat.

What Eon Will You Awaken?

Gulin said, "'Not to notice [the ultimate] when it's raised is off the mark. If you try to ponder and judge, what eon will you awaken?' If all of you can practice according to this, then you will be given the bequest. Do you understand?

"Only after the snow has weighed them down do we know the strength of the pines. Only when things are difficult do we see people's hearts."

Among the Herd

On the anniversary of Buddha's enlightenment, Gulin said:

"When one moon is in the sky, its reflections are contained in the myriad waters. When one cataract is in the eye, optical illusions cascade in confusion. Old Shakyamuni ran in among a herd of water buffalo.

"Thus it is said, 'Attain it from Mind, and the noxious becomes fragrant. Lose it in ideation, and the sweet dew is then a garden of brambles.'"

* ───

> *Old Shakyamuni ran in among a herd of buffalo* in order to communicate enlightenment to people locked up inside their socially sanctioned illusions, who were not ready to listen to his message.

Complacency

Gulin said, "Today is the twentieth day of the last month of the year. We better exchange our complacency for urgency. Don't let the year end with you discussing things and not measuring up to being patch-robed monks. When you must walk, walk; when you must sit, sit—what's there to discuss?" Gulin held his staff upright and said, "The frog cannot jump out of the basket."

* ───

> *The frog* of intellect cannot jump out of *the basket* of conditioning.

Options

Gulin said, "Ordinary people reify [the phenomenal world] and think it exists in the absolute sense. Those who seek enlightenment separate from the world, reject it, and think it does not exist. Those enlightened through contemplation of the causal nexus think is exists like an illusion. For bodhisattvas, right in its embodiment it is emptiness.

"In the scriptures Buddha says, 'If anyone sees me in terms of form or seeks for me in terms of sound, this person is following a false path and cannot see me.'"

The Bridge Is Flowing, Not the Water

Gulin said:

> Empty handed, holding a hoe.
> Midnight, passing by the city.
> Going on foot, astride a water buffalo.
> Wandering on the deep sea bottom.
> People are passing over the bridge,
> Dragging along oxen and millstones.
> The bridge is flowing, not the water.
> In the tree we hang a lamp.

What Dharma?

Up in the hall Gulin said, "Before I ever ascended to this seat, the ancient Buddha Kashyapa had already mentioned it to all of you. But tell me, what Dharma did he talk about?

"Two don't break into one: the One Dharma remains secure forever. If you understand in terms of unity versus duality, you will sink down in karmic suffering for endless ages."

Suddenly he held up his staff and said, "Supporting us as we cross Broken Bridge River, it accompanies us as we return to Bright Moon Village."

* ──

In Zen lore, the prehistoric *Buddha Kashyapa* was one of the seven ancient buddhas considered to have predated Shakyamuni Buddha, the historical "founder" of Buddhism.

The Family Style

Upon inaugurating his second stay at Kaiyuan Temple in Pingjiang-fu, Gulin said:

"In a later-day movement of the reduplicating array of light, we again turn the Dharma Wheel. We propagate the family style of the old days: we do not fall into the ruts of the present. Straightaway, clouds come and rain falls: where the water goes, a channel forms. Not only does it add to the sparkle of the stones in the streams: even humans and celestial beings take delight.

"One phrase encompasses the five thousand volumes of the scriptures. The myriad mental impulses suddenly arrive at the stage of being crystal clear on all sides.

"The pure wind circles the earth, the glowing sun is in the sky. One Path empty and solid: far flung light and color.

"How is it at just such a time? Inside the boundaries, the sun and moon are hung vertical and horizontal. Outside the conventional square, heaven and earth roll up and roll out as they will."

A Living Road to Share

Gulin said, "In the scriptural teachings it says that if a single person generates true intent and returns to the origin, then all of space in the ten directions crumbles away. The ancestral teachers of Zen said that if there is a single person who generates true intent and returns to the origin, then he bumps into [the ultimate] at every turn.

"Here at Kaiyuan Temple I have a living road that I will walk along with all of you."

Then Gulin slapped the meditation bench and said, "One gust of the west wind, two or three pounds of fallen leaves."

* ───

One gust of the west wind, two or three pounds of fallen leaves: The teacher presents the teaching in a public forum, a handful of people in the audience are reached.

Natural Patterns

Gulin said, "Good people, the ancients were like wind blowing across the water, naturally forming patterns. As for the people of today, if you just look within the standard texts, what connection will there be [to the true message]? When I report to you like this, what do you make of it?"

After a silence Gulin said, "Good roots are the same everywhere under heaven."

* ───

Good roots: The basic behavioral patterns of generosity, discipline, patience, and dedication that lay the basis for awakening.

Preaching the Dharma

To the monk in charge of guests [whose duties included giving basic lessons on Buddhism to visitors to the temple], Gulin said:

"Never blind the eyes of sentient beings—you should rather have your body pulverized to atoms.

"Ahead are the great bodhisattvas Avalokiteshvara and Maha-sthamaprapta, behind are the great bodhisattvas Manjushri and Samantabhadra. On the right are the horse-faced soldiers, on the left are the bull-headed guardians of hell. Flames are in the middle.

"You preach the Dharma for all the buddhas of past, present, and future, and all the buddhas of past, present, and future stand there and listen.

"If they can understand, host and guest switch, and ordinary and holy interchange. Birth, death, going, coming—it's like wandering through a garden sightseeing.

"If they do not understand, no one lives in a broken down house, so let the prairie fire burn it down!"

* ———————————————————————————————

Great bodhisattvas: Avalokiteshvara, associated with compassion for the world; Mahasthamaprapta, who represents the power of wisdom; Manjushri, identified with transcendent wisdom; and Samantabhadra, who embodies the universal mission of bodhisattvas working for enlightenment in all worlds.

Horse-faced soldiers, bull-headed guardians: Fearsome images often present in East Asian Buddhist temples representing supernatural protectors of the teaching of truth.

To Help You People

Gulin said, "It is said that with the path of the enlightened teachers, it is a great fault to bring it up alone, and it is a great fault to speak of buddhas and Zen masters. I disagree. When I bring it up alone, it is to help all you people, and when I speak of buddhas and Zen masters, it is to help all you people.

"The World-Honored One said, 'If you suppose there is anything that goes beyond nirvana, I would say that this too is like a dream, like an illusion.'"

Homage to a Teacher

On the anniversary of the death of his teacher Master Hengchuan, Gulin held up incense and said:

"Before he was born, this old fellow was coarse and crude. Nobody in the world could do anything about him. After he died, he was fatheaded and dull. Everywhere spirits wailed and ghosts wept.

"Thus it is said, 'He's like this living and he's like this dying—he sheers through iron and cuts through nails without anything to hold him back.'

"This morning I specially dedicate a brazier of incense to him. I hear a donkey bray and it cuts into my guts."

Host and Guest

A monk asked, "What is guest within guest?" Gulin said, "When they meet, they make scrupulous efforts."

"What is host within guest?" Gulin said, "Riding a donkey into the noisy marketplace."

"What is guest within host?" Gulin said, "His whole face is covered with dust."

"What is host within host?" Gulin said, "From east to west without companions."

* ───────────────────────────────────────

The *guest* represents conditioned perception and the relative world as perceived through it; the ordinary social personality, the mind of delusion, the body of affliction and defilement.

The *host* stands for enlightened awareness and reality-as-it-is, where absolute and relative are fused, and nirvana and birth-and-death are not two; the true self, the Buddha-Mind, the body of liberation and purity.

Elegance

Gulin said, "When I press on it, the ocean-seal emits light. When you agitate your minds, sensory afflictions have already arisen. Look! Look! Old Shakyamuni opened up all the doors at once.

"What obstructs you is not a [physical] wall—the place you get through is not [physically] empty. If you can pass through, you walk alone through the crimson clouds. If you cannot pass through, you are submerged in the dead water. Thus it is said: 'If your mentality does not leave its position, you fall into a poison sea. If your mind does not deviate, the myriad things are one suchness.'

"At the monastery gate we join our palms; in the buddha-shrine we burn incense. On the top of the flagpole we turn flips; on the brink of a mile high cliff we play ball. When there is will and energy, we add will and energy, so where it's elegant it is even more elegant."

* ────────────────────────────────

If your mentality does not leave its position, you fall into a poison sea: If you stay absorbed in emptiness or any meditative state, this becomes an attachment in itself.

If your mind does not deviate, the myriad things are one suchness: If your conditioned mind does not go into action creating dualistic perception, then the unity of the myriad things and the one reality is experienced directly.

Fishing for Enlightenment

Gulin said, "In our world the sentient beings have three kinds of suffering, namely, craving, anger, and ignorance. They cast off bodies and take on bodies, appearing here and disappearing there, falsely accepting the sensory experience they cling to and all sorts of afflictions. The buddhas of past, present, and future are compassionate and happy to give forth their ultimate skillful means.

They leave Tushita Heaven and come down to be born on earth and manifest excellent qualities amid the sensory afflictions here.

"Yunmen said, 'When there are no sticking points in what meets the eye, then you reach the point where named and categorized things and all phenomena are empty. "Mountains," "rivers," "the great earth"—these are names. When names cannot be found—this is called samadhi. The ocean of reality is fully equipped with everything, but this is still a wave swirling around without a wind. Just forget your supposed knowledge in awakening. Awakening is buddha-nature. [When you awaken,] you are called an unconcerned person. But you still must come to know the one transcendent opening.'

"How is it at just such a time? When you're at home you say it will be easy, but when you're out there with the fishing pole you finally realize that catching fish is hard."

* ───

> *Tushita Heaven:* In Buddhist cosmology, a heaven where enlightened beings dwell before being reborn on earth.

The Path

Gulin said, "Having no conditioned mind is the Path: the Path is fundamentally mindless. Abandon the false and seek the true: the true is the original basis for the false. Take empty space as the true body, and it appears whole in everything. Take the whole earth as a meditation bench, and you fit the groove everywhere.

"Thus it is said, 'The Dharma is practiced according to the Dharma. The Dharma banner is established according to the place.'

"The Zen master's staff divides the world horizontally. The Zen traveler's straw sandals break through heaven and earth. The absolute truth is clear on the tips of a hundred grasses, suddenly revealing the grasp of a patch-robed monk. If you plant beans, when will you ever get rice?"

* ───────────────────────────────

> *You fit the groove everywhere:* A classical metaphor for the ability of an enlightened person to make the right move spontaneously at the right time.
>
> *The Dharma banner:* The Dharma, the teaching of enlightenment, has inherent norms; the *Dharma banner,* meaning the way the teaching is expressed, depends on the mentality of the audience, the time and the place.
>
> *The grasp of a patch-robed monk:* The mastery of a Zen adept who sees the true nature of the phenomenal world, and experiences the fusion of the absolute and the relative.
>
> *If you plant beans, when will you ever get rice?* If you dedicate your energy to pursuing the motivations of the false self, how can you awaken to the Buddhist path?

A Living Shore

Gulin said, "In the intimate encounter with an enlightened teacher, there's a living shore—what's so hard to see?

"Quick, focus your eyes and see the immortal. Don't look at the fan in the immortal's hand."

* ───────────────────────────────

> *Focus your eyes and see the immortal. Don't look at the fan in the immortal's hand:* Wake up to your buddha-nature, don't get fixated on the means by which the teacher is pointing it out.

The Teachings
of Zhuxian

Arrival

The night before Zhuxian entered Nanzenji Temple there was heavy rain and thunder. Near dawn the sky cleared.

As he arrived at the temple gate, Zhuxian said:

> One peal of thunder shakes ten thousand layers of clouds.
> The sun shines in the eternal sky as rain pours down,
> Washing out the green mountains—boundless good!
> Riding backward on an iron horse, I ascend to the Dragon
>   Gate.

* ───

Nanzenji Temple is in Kyoto, Japan.

One peel of thunder represents the Buddhist message; the *layers of clouds* stand for the conditioning in which sentient beings are encased.

Riding backward on an iron horse: Riding on the power of imperturbable wisdom into infinity, looking back into the world of ordinary reality.

Words for the Shogun

Burning the incense offered by the supreme warlord Ashikaga Takauji, Zhuxian said:

"I humbly hope that it may be for you as it was for the Duke of Zhou, that the common people yearn for you to extend your rule to them. I hope that without resorting to military force, you can bring about Great Peace."

Burning the incense offered by the warlord Ashikaga Tadayoshi, Zhuxian said:

"I humbly hope that you meet the Source left and right and mesh with the groove high and low, and your capacity encompasses countless worlds. If you are a true patron of Buddhism, your virtue harmonizes with heaven and earth and you are like a loving parent to the common people."

* ————————————————————————————

The Ashikaga brothers *Takauji* and *Tadayoshi* were the most powerful military overlords in the fragmented feudal society of Japan at the time.

The Duke of Zhou was one of the Confucian paragons of an enlightened ruler.

Words for the Zen Monks

At a small gathering at the end of the summer retreat, Zhuxian said:

"Tomorrow morning concludes our retreat. At tonight's small gathering, what shall we talk about? The Buddhist scriptures? Bodhi and nirvana? True Thusness and liberation? Everything that the generations of the world's great teachers have already spoken of in every possible way?

"These are all scraps of food left over from countless sacrifices, a cud that's been spit up countless times. Only starving dogs would taste it. Humans would hold their noses—how could they eat it?

"We say that these are 'not the words of the time,' that they are irrelevant [for now], that they are various kinds of poison.

"If you have full certainty, then you can slay buddhas and patriarchs as you meet them twenty-four hours a day, and when you meet yourself, you slay yourself. Only after that is everything up to you, whatever you do. As the saying goes, 'To preserve life, one must slay [the false self]. When it is completely slain, only then can you abide in peace.' If you don't slay it, then you can't move an inch—a blade of grass is hard to move and a drop of water is hard to digest.

"Some say that the spine under a monk's robe should not be put down just anywhere; whether still or moving, he must not take it easy in any of his actions. Those who talk this kind of talk do so to draw in those of you with beginners' potential. It's like chewing up food first to feed it to infants. [Those who only present the elementary level of Buddhism] do not realize how shameless they're being.

"If we speak of the part of us that's fundamental: it's empty, yet it functions, and it has room for you to stand too. What's more, it even talks to you about your good points and shortcomings and prods you along. What's important is that you must recognize your fundamental identity. If you make your plans for living in the ghost cave [of the false self and its conditioned subjectivity], what could be so special?

"Yesterday I first entered this temple. Today it is already time to conclude the summer retreat. Human affairs are so hurried—we let the time slip by. As I look upon this assembly, I see that all of you are high-class guests in the Dragon Gate. This is why our Bodhidharma came to China, observing from afar that there were vessels with the potential for the Great Vehicle there. Since every one of you already holds within him such a vessel, how could you return to your petty knowledge and small views and wrap your-selves up in them?

"Dahui said, 'Everywhere else they talk snail Zen, convoluted and twisted. Here at my place it's oyster Zen—as soon as he opens his mouth, you see his guts.'

"I am not this way. I have no snail Zen, and no oyster Zen either. Within a hundred and twenty days of drinking the water, you will know the source for yourself."

The Moon

Zhuxian said, "One moon is in the sky. Its reflections are con-tained in the myriad streams of water. All of space in all directions, mountains, rivers, and the whole earth, the whole dense array of myriad forms, humans, animals, and all types of things—these are reflections. All the actions of living beings, their comings and goings and all their movements, their seeing and hearing and feel-ing and knowing, all the thousands of transformations of sentient and insentient—these are all reflections. But where is the moon? Is there anyone who recognizes the moon?"

This Mind

Zhuxian said, "Everyone, it's just This Mind. Every mind is bud-dha. It's not vertical or horizontal. It has no front or back. It has no going or coming, no birth or demise.

"Thus, [in This Mind] where there is no coming or going, no birth or demise, the sages manifest all kinds of forms and do all kinds of things. They establish the power of virtue and apply humane methods to bring order to the world. They impart standards and set up teachings to transform the people in their millions. The sages are as upright and illustrious as heaven—their spiritual achievements go beyond the world. Even the mountain forests and the grassy fields receive their benevolence. Sun and moon, heaven and earth, return together to their path.

"Haven't you read what Shanhui said? 'There's something before heaven and earth, formless and fundamentally still. It can act as the master of the myriad forms. It doesn't wither with the seasons.'

"This 'something' is none other than Mind. Ordinarily, it's mind, but when we witness [its reality], it's called 'buddha.' It's also called Dharmakaya, the buddha's body of reality, and it's also called 'the highest meaning of the holy truths.'

"Only this one is real—everything else is not. It does not block people at all—the One Path leads out of birth-and-death. The bodies of all the buddhas are just this one body of reality, this Dharmakaya."

* ──

Shanhui (805–881): A Zen teacher who worked at Mount Jiashan. The story goes that Shanhui was enlightened when his teacher, a Zen monk known as "The Boatman," threw him into the river.

On with the Show

Zhuxian held up a summons from the emperor and said, "This has come down from the Ninth Heaven. It's a rope through my nose. As I'm being pulled off by it, I leave it to one of my assistants to test your strong points and shortcomings."

After a question and answer period, Zhuxian said:

"[Xuefeng said,] 'Pick up all of heaven and earth and compress it to the size of a grain of rice.'

"Inside this grain of rice, I am running all over the world. I was intending to go to some other world, but now the shogun has memorialized the emperor, who has sent down an imperial summons insisting that I return here again, that I follow the thread again, that I assume my formal deportment again, and again beat the drum and play the flute on stage, and work the puppets from inside the puppet-stage. Though I am the same man as before, they want to see a new-style dance."

* ———————————————————————————————

Ninth Heaven: The highest heaven in the folk cosmology of medieval China. Here Zhuxian is referring to the abode of the emperor of Japan.

The shogun has memorialized the emperor: In Japan at this time, the shogun held real power, but maintained a façade of deference to the emperor, asking his permission in certain matters. Here the shogun requested that the emperor command Zhuxian to return to Nanzenji Temple.

Etiquette Monks

The etiquette-monks just keep on coming:
Etiquette-monks last year, etiquette-monks this year,
Etiquette-monks yesterday, etiquette-monks today.
Year after year the etiquette-monks keep coming,
Day after day the etiquette-monks arrive.
The etiquette-monks have their etiquette,
But they don't realize they go back and forth in vain.
As I face great disaster, behind me there's uproarious
    laughter.
As I stand on the precipice, in front of me hands try
    to pull me over.
Not only do they try to pull me over—
After I've fallen they hammer me with rock.
There are some who sympathize with me—
They have mouths, but they cannot open them.

They see me, then depart;

Between us there's a feeling of emptiness and grief.

Alas, the etiquette-monks keep coming—

Who among them sees [beyond etiquette] to our duty to
   the truth?

Bubbles

Zhuxian said, "Fundamentally, birth is not birth, and death is not death. Birth, death, going, coming—a bubble pops, a bubble arises. Thus it is said: 'All compounded phenomena are like dreams, like illusions, like bubbles, like reflections, like dew, like lightning.' You should view things like this."

One Great Purpose

Zhuxian said, "You must realize that all the buddhas appeared in the world for one great purpose: they wanted to enable sentient beings to open up their enlightened perception.

"When you enter into enlightened perception, it is like the sun at high noon. Its light shines on everything, on high and low equally, so every nook and cranny is illuminated.

"The purpose of the buddhas was not to have people attain nirvana in isolation. Rather, they led people to nirvana with the nirvana of the tathagatas [which includes compassionate action and uncontrived wisdom].

"They dispensed expedient teachings correctly and directly, and only expounded the supreme path. They used all kinds of metaphors and countless explanations so that all sentient beings could be opened to enlightenment and enter into the perception of the buddhas, so that they could advance in their practice without retreating, benefiting self and others, practicing the perfection of giving the Dharma."

The True Person

Forty-two years, all a great dream
The permutations of logic are all empty sounds
Last night dead, this morning alive
The true person without position walks in the fire

*　——————————————————————————————————

> The true person without position: The real self. Linji said, "In this lump of red flesh, there's a true person without position constantly going in and out through the gates of the senses."

Coming and Going

At an observance to mark the death of a prominent Buddhist layman known as Zosen, Zhuxian said:

"Coming forth in birth, going in with death, revealing alone the workings of reality. Showing being, showing nothingness, manifesting all the reflections and echoes. Thus it is said: 'Coming, coming, but not really coming; going, going, but not really going.'

"Cut off coming and going, and do not dwell in between—then body and mind are in nirvana. The everywhere-equal fundamental reality perfectly fills the ten directions and extends through countless worlds.

"[Real Buddhist adepts] must know how to dwell without abiding anywhere. Possessed of the pure body of reality, they manifest transformation bodies by means of deeds that are like illusions. They come to dwell in past, present, and future without change—their bodies are not bodies, their minds and bodies are like empty space. Their practice is unobstructed and transcends the worldly eye.

"Good people, do you see Layman Zosen in this? Look, look! Right now his eyelashes reach across the ten directions and his eyebrows extend through heaven and earth above and the underworld below. Forever in profound clarity, he is not apart from here and now.

"If you search for him, I'll know you cannot see."

* ———————————————————————————————————————

> *Transformation bodies and the body of reality:* The enlightened all share one formless essence, called the truth-body, or the body of reality (Dharmakaya). To communicate with sentient beings, the enlightened appear in an infinite variety of forms, called transformation bodies, or emanation bodies (Nirmanakaya).

Look Carefully

In the presence of the retired emperor Hanazono, Zhuxian said:

"Good people, look carefully at the smoke from the incense as it rises. Right this moment all the countless millions of billions of buddhas and enlightened teachers in all worlds are arrayed here before you. From their different mouths, the same voice speaks a verse:

> From dragons follow clouds
> From tigers, wind
> The sages act
> The myriad beings look on

"Having spoken this verse, each of them goes into inconceivable samadhi such that the countless millions of billions of buddhas and enlightened teachers in all worlds, and all the countless worlds themselves, all reflect each other and enter into each other, without holding back from each other and without obstructing each other.

"This is what is called empty but aware, quiescent but wonder-working, without abiding, without dependence—that which every-thing rests on, transcending everything but without leaving everything behind. Do all of you see this?"

Then Zhuxian picked up his whisk and drew a circle in the air, saying, "Right now everything is in here. The right time is hard to meet, and sages are hard to encounter. Better take advantage of this occasion. If you have any doubts, I invite you to ask questions."

The Coming from the West

A monk asked, "What was the meaning of the coming from the west?"

Zhuxian said, "To make you ask."

* ————————————————————

The coming from the west: Bodhidharma coming from India to China with the Zen transmission.

This is a traditional question in the Zen schools, to which many answers were given through the ages.

What Are We Studying Here?

At a small gathering Zhuxian said, "Tomorrow morning we wrap up the summer retreat. At tonight's small gathering, ten thousand words are not as good as having one's own power.

"The whole world is the temple of complete enlightenment. What are we concluding here? There is not the slightest thing that is not everywhere equal inherent wisdom. What are we studying here? Each and every person has head to the sky and feet to the ground, and goes beyond the buddhas and patriarchs.

"[True reality] is like water moving in the earth—it's everywhere. When it comes to light as ponds and wells and rivers and streams, it surges up to flood the sun and the sky. There is not a single thing that does not receive its benefits. When a channel is opened to the east, it flows to the east, and when a channel is opened to the west, it flows to the west.

"It's all up to the individual person."

Good and Evil

At the Stupa for the Benefit of Living Beings in Kamakura, Zhuxian said:

"Evil can lead to the opening of the gate of countless merits. When evil is eliminated, countless merits are achieved. As we contemplate this magnificent precious stupa, we see that innumerable situations are really like this. What was formerly a horrific battlefield has now been transformed into a forest of merit.

"The two conditioning causes, good and evil, have no basis—they are entirely within the mind-ground of sentient beings. Once the thorny brambles that grow so high are cut away, the wondrous flowers of enlightenment bloom and fill the tree.

"So too with the Dharmakaya of all the buddhas. It's just a matter of realization amid the empty body of illusory transformation: subtly entering birthlessness where nothing is not born, subtly cutting off formlessness with nothing not formed, transcending the triple world, having no location and yet responding readily to the myriad forms of being, with no more comparative awareness."

* ———————————————————————————————

Comparative awareness: Perception based on comparison with an inventory of preconceived categories. Enlightenment is marked by immediate awareness, direct perception.

New Year's Day

On New Year's Day, after answering questions, Zhuxian said:

"This morning it is the first day of the first month. Gradually we see the wind of harmony gently, almost imperceptibly blowing on the root of the flower of original beauty.

"The myriad things all share one substance. Thus it is said: 'Genuine, straightforward, without falsity—this is the mind of a person of the Path.' Mind and Path are the same, ancient and modern are the same, everything in the world is the same. We reach the summit on a thousand peaks and face the source in ten thousand streams."

Then Zhuxian cited a saying of Yunmen's: "A monk asked, 'What is talk that goes beyond the buddhas and patriarchs?' Yunmen said, 'Cake.'

"Good people, today is New Year's Day. We have taken charge of these unexcelled royal provisions."

Buddhism in Decline

Zhuxian wrote:

"Here in the last part of the Semblance Period, Buddhism is gradually declining. Human hearts are pallid and indifferent. Outstanding people are hard to find—the Zen gate is silent and desolate. How Zen has declined in comparison with the earlier adepts!

"In these times, if we want to look for the right people for Zen, they must have spirit bones from past lives, and have the power of great vows, and ride the wheels of great practice, in order to travel the Great Path free from inversion and error. Why? In these times when the trend is a world in decline, the road appears ever more twisted and convoluted. Worldly forms are inordinately chaotic and worn out, while desire for worldly profit is thick and flourishing.

"Thus worldly affairs have a great influence over people, who are sure to be carried off by worldly things if their roots are superficial and their power is shallow, if their practices and vows are not profound, and if they are not completely upright in their inner hearts. Once they carry people off, worldly things become a barrier that seals people in, and they cannot escape it even for a minute. People just go on with their petty work—the unworthy mind has no other plan, it just wants to profit and nurture itself and outdo others in glory, that's all.

"[Supposedly religious people] join together with their cronies and form sects for the deluded, factions of devils. If you enter the religious life for these reasons, will your body and mind actually be at peace? Once people have solidified their delusions, all that they say and do will be the business of delusion. Since at root their theories are not correct, the things they do miss the mark from the start. If you fall among this type, even if you have some knowledge, what real use will it be?"

*   ————————————————————————————

> The Semblance Period: The period in the history of Buddhism when the outward forms of belief and practice still remain, but have lost their effectiveness as aids to enlightenment.

Two Verses

"Buddha Dharma"—two words very easy to say.
I only fear that no one will pay attention and listen.
Focus your ears and hear the night rain.
Don't let yourself not wake up with us.
"Buddha Dharma"—two words impossible to say.
Don't be surprised as my mouth opens lazily.
Focus your tongue as you swallow a grain of rice.
When you're free and at ease, how could you slander
    the Tathagata?

Pure Land Poems

The Guide reaches out his hand to receive us,
But we act crazy and run away.
Our basic real identity is nothing but the Buddha-Mind,
    all sufficient.
It has never lacked anything.
Heaven rains down jewel flowers to cover the jade ground.
The music of the immortals blows on the wind as we cross
    the golden pond.
Day after day the Real People wave to beckon us,
Watching for us to bridle the ox of self-satisfaction.
To return to our old home so pure and serene.
We don't need a magic vessel to hide in,
The road is in the inherent nature of our own minds.
Eyes open, eyes closed, it is never forgotten.
Buddha is not far distant from us.
Holding Buddha in our hearts, we should be generous and
    expansive.
Precious lotus flowers we offer at his golden feet,
Twenty-four hours a day on the tips of our noses.

*

Real People: Originally a Taoist term for those who have unified the Mind of the Tao with their human minds, or in Buddhist terms, awakened their inherent potential for enlightened perception, so that they can function in the ordinary world without losing touch with absolute reality.

A Warning

In an afterword to a collection of Zen sayings, Zhuxian wrote:

"Zen teachers respond to the world. All their recorded sayings are the meanings bequeathed by the buddhas and ancestral teachers. For the sake of the one great matter [of opening the enlightened perception], they had no choice but to resort to words and phrases. When they press down or lift up, when they praise or blame, when they appear or disappear freely, it is not mere word-play. It is all pure gold and prime jade that has been refined until it is completely flawless.

"What sort of people are those who are ignorant of this, who usurp the name of Zen teacher and compose collections of sayings? Even at the verbal level, their learning is incomplete, yet they play this game!

"Perhaps some of them are really enlightened teachers, so that what they do is guide beings according to what is appropriate to them—I do not know. But for those who are not, since their causal basis is not genuine, the results they bring about will be twisted. When these twisted results appear, things do not go as they wish in their present lifetimes, and probably when they die they will enter into dark paths and their karmic consciousness will receive its reward: they will fall into uninterrupted hell, with no escape. Or if they do escape hell, they will come back as rats.

"Regret is always too late! I respectfully warn you younger people to devote your whole strength and will to learn all about the business of the sages. Even if you have investigated it completely, always keep the sense that you have not yet arrived—only this will do.

"As for those of scanty merit with no hope of enlightenment, and their worthless word-play, and their claims of attainment when they have no attainment and of realization when they have no realization—how can we bear to do nothing? We must warn them to stop."

A Visit to the Immortals

To visit the immortals, you don't need to go to their abode
  on Mount Penglai.
The ocean road to the edge of the sky is so vast and boundless,
But the flying cart surely does not fear the distance.
Right now Penglai dwells among humans.
When I tell you this, won't you give a sigh of relief?
It saves you the trouble and pounding of a long journey.
The worldly say that the River of the Immortals is thirty thou-
  sand miles away.
But if it's really right here, how could it be so hard to reach?
This road cannot be measured,
This mountain is not a pointed spire.
I have enjoyed this story,
Singing in exaltation, traveling alone across pure rivers
  and bays.
The river is broad, the swimming fish a chaotic, countless
  multitude.
They seem to hear my song and gather in a bunch.
I beat out another measure of my song and they begin to leap
  about again.
I sigh in wonder that the fish are so wise while the humans
  are so obstinately stupid.
Me singing, the fish swimming—it's all one design.
The fishes' mind, my intent—they're not two.
The fish can listen to the song and hear the words.
The words?—ten thousand rebukes to urge you on.
Sometimes saying: a snail dwells in a hole so narrow.
Sometimes saying: a dragon emerges from the sea so broad.
Sometimes saying: the world of the dusts is noisy and chaotic.
Sometimes saying: the realm of the immortals is pure and
  peaceful.

Now I'm speaking, other times I'm silent.

The fish come out to swim like this—why should they return?

Finished listening to the words, the fish leave and listen no more.

I observe the fish—they're already empty—there's no observing.

Crossing the wave to plumb the depths, searching for the
   trackless,

I only see a strange monolith shaped like a pointed mountain.

Its shape is more dangerous, more singular than Penglai.

Its sheer cliffs tower up, its pure streams plummet down.

From then on I have the bluegreen ocean inside my shirt.

Then I know this land is not the world of men.

In the renowned garden on high, the peaches are planted.

Long branches with tiny buds extend in profusion.

Red and white, fragrant for a season,

Resplendent in the warm sun, how could they endure cold
   winds?

What surpassing beauty in the colors of spring across the
   continents!

When their allotted timespan is up, we see the flowers fade.

How much better to find a magical stone:

Coldly it faces us—a visage of eternal joy.

Right now Penglai is the human world.

What I said before was not a lie.

I've always felt sorry for you, because you don't have enough
   "food" to sustain you.

This is why you make offerings—you hope to forget your hunger.

I wonder if these days you know how to eat your fill or not.

The ice bowl and the water dipper are musty from disuse.

*　───────────────────────────────────────

   Mount Penglai: In Taoist lore, the abode of the Immortals, pictured
   as an remote island in the ocean. The *River of the Immortals* flows
   from it.

The Teachings
of Daian

Still in Effect

Daian held up the imperial order appointing him abbot of Yunju Temple and said:

"The bequest on Spirit Peak still has its effect today. The Buddha Dharma pervades all-under-heaven, the Imperial Benevolence is never ending."

* —————————————————————————————

The bequest on Spirit Peak: The mind-to-mind transmission of Zen communicated through the generations from Buddha.

An Echo in Space

Daian said:

"The Tao is before your eyes, but what's before your eyes is not the Tao. Those who are deluded, delude themselves. Those who awaken, awaken themselves. There is no room to hesitate in thought—how could it involve verbal explanations?

"Just be able to empty through and forget objects of attachment. Then naturally, wherever you touch, the Tao will be revealed.

"Even if you can quote ancient and modern and talk of mysteries and wonders and with great artifice offer up devices and rationalizations and stir the Zen wind, I say that this is all upside-down delusion and false thought.

"The Tao was passed down from buddha to buddha and transmitted from enlightened teacher to enlightened teacher. Viewed with the correct eye, though, this was picking up empty space to catch an echo."

Suddenly Daian held up the staff and called out to the assembly, "Today at Yunju Temple there is no alternative: I've scored another defeat. Thirty years from now surely someone will come along to check it out."

He planted the staff upright and said, "The upsweep of the thousand peaks stops at the colossal backbone of the range, the sounds of the ten thousand streams dissolve when they return to the ocean."

* ———————————————————————————————————

> *The Tao is before your eyes, but what's before your eyes is not the Tao*: All that faces us is a manifestation of the one reality, but what we actually perceive is based on our conditioning and the categories we impose on reality.
>
> *Picking up empty space to catch an echo*: Functioning within the illusory world to save illusory beings. In this sense Daian too has *scored another defeat*, because as a Zen teacher he has no alternative but to give provisional expression to a truth that is ultimately inexpressible.

Restoration Work

Daian had organized the restoration of the ruined temple at Yunju. When the old foundation of the temple had been uncovered, Daian said to the assembly:

"Yesterday we cleared the wild ground. We asked all of you to cut away the brambles and remove the rubble. The original foundation has already been clearly revealed. In the middle is a tree that no one has been able to uproot.

"Today I cannot avoid employing another expedient: with my sharp sword I cut away the tangled branches and leaves and with my blunt hoe I chop out the roots of misguided delusion. The work on the ground of reality fuses into one whole: the abbot's axe leaves no marks."

Beware of False Teachers

Daian taught the assembly:

"Those who act as teachers of the Zen school have no choice but to impart a word or half a phrase. It is all done to pull out nails and extract pegs for learners, to melt the sticking points and remove the bonds. Those who are good at wielding the great sword of wisdom naturally do not cut their own hands on it.

"In recent generations those who occupy the teacher's place and instruct students hold to memorized texts and admire decorative verbiage: they dazzle younger people with their boasts and cause bad habits to increase. Not knowing of the existence of the road for the true self to emerge on, they put on fine silk to walk through a forest of thorns. They cannot get free. With these false teachers, the school of direct pointing, the school of Bodhidharma, has fallen to the ground. How painful indeed!

"The denizens of the sea must have eyes as they travel about, lest they fall into someone else's net and be unable to emerge. As the ancients said, 'To enter this gate, do not keep interpretive knowledge.' But in my view, even if your interpretive knowledge is suddenly forgotten, you are still somebody outside the gate.

"To succeed when you get here, you must distinguish black from plain, religious from ordinary.

"Take care!"

They put on fine silk to walk through a forest of thorns: They assume a veneer of Buddhist learning to pursue a life of worldly ambitions.

You must distinguish black from plain: Zen monks wore black, in contrast to the plain homespun of the peasants. But accurately distinguishing religious from ordinary cannot be done by depending on externals—as in Daian's time, there have always been numerous people in religious garb pursuing purely worldly motivations, as well as genuine adepts with no signs of outward religiosity about them.

Today

At the end of the summer retreat, Daian said, "The holy period is now complete. It is precisely Today. At other teaching centers they speak of Zen and the Path and make a lot of noise. Here we are solitary and far transcendent, lofty and steep. Even if the Buddha Dharma is present, who will set eyes on it and look?"

Then Daian slapped the meditation bench and left his seat.

Precisely Today: Conventional ideas of time are part of the structure of conditioned perception. From the transcendent point of view, past, present, and future are all simultaneously present, all visible from an eternal Today of direct perception outside of time and space. Zen teachers often used *Today* to mean the day of enlightenment.

Let the Snow Melt Away

A monk asked, "What is my true self?"

Daian said, "Who is making you ask like this?"

The monk bowed in homage.

Then Daian said, "[As the saying goes,] 'If you do not understand the Tao is what meets the eye, then how will you know the road to walk on?' It seems that when he talked like this, the man of old labored in vain. As for my view, I want all of you to know it."

Daian suddenly lifted his staff and brandished it once and said, "Just let the snow melt away: then naturally spring arrives." Then he left the teacher's seat.

* ───────────────────────────────────────

Who is making you ask like this? It is our latent potential for enlightenment, our long forgotten but undying link with the absolute, that impels us to seek the path to enlightenment.

Let the snow of delusion melt away, and the springtime of enlightened perception arrives by itself.

Turning Words

One day two monks asked Daian for instruction.

To one of the monks Daian posed this question: "The whole world is the person's self: where does he put his eyes, ears, nose, tongue, body, and intellect?" The monk said nothing.

Then Daian asked the second monk: "Mount Sumeru is smashing your skull to bits: why don't you feel the pain?" This monk also said nothing.

Daian turned to his attendant and said, "Record these two turning words."

* ───────────────────────────────────────

Turning words are sayings that reveal multiple layers of meaning as they interact with the mind of the person who contemplates them.

For the two turning words here, a hint at the first level:

Since in essence we are at one with the world, how can we deploy our perception so that it does not function dualistically and put us at odds with the world?

Why don't we feel the pain our attachment to the phenomenal world (*Mount Sumeru*) brings us?

The Ancient Road

Daian said, "Flecks of clouds, murmuring waters, thousands and thousands of mountains filling the eyes. The mountains' visage is serene and still, the birds call in harmony.

"In front of the gate the ancient road is flat as a fine whetstone— it does not go back and forth with the people of the time."

Bringing Forth a Sutra from an Atom of Dust

Once when the monk in charge of instructing the laiety returned to the temple from a teaching trip, Daian said:

"The Zen man has been away teaching and now has returned. Entering the gate with a laugh, he extends his excess compassion. Smashing open an atom of dust, he brings forth a great sutra. He beats the drum and rings the bell and announces it to everyone.

"Tell me, at precisely this moment, where does the merit go back to?

"Last night spring returned beyond the Empty Eon. The perfume of the flower of awakening seeps from branches that have not yet sprouted."

Awaiting a Worthy Successor

Once when it was snowing Daian said, "The earth is covered with snow. Here deep in the mountains it's extra cold. If a worthy successor had not arrived, Bodhidharma's facing a wall would have been for no reason.

"But tell me, everyone: did Bodhidharma have no reason? Do I have no reason?"

Daian held up the staff, then threw it down and said, "No reason, no reason."

Bodhidharma's facing a wall: The story goes that Bodhidharma sat facing a wall in his retreat in North China for years, not speaking to anyone, awaiting the arrival of someone capable of preserving the Zen teaching intact. When his future successor did at last arrive, Bodhidharma let him wait all night as the snow piled up around the two of them.

Temple Scene

Daian said:

"Today is the fifteenth day of the first month. Monks and laymen are thronging around the temple gate. As soon as the attendants put a roof over the teaching hall, followers of the Path beat the Dharma drum. The old monk comes out in a wild hurry: what spare time is there to quote and discuss ancients and moderns? His whole life he has criticized all the Zen centers, and today it's another scene of coarse confusion.

"Everyone—though coarse confusion is not lacking, to get anywhere, you still must know the time and recognize what's appropriate. It is better to pretend to be mute and deaf and look on dispassionately at their rustic songs and dances round the altar."

Rustic songs and dances: Though the emotional fervor of the crowd of believers has nothing to do with Zen itself, Daian tolerates it because he recognizes what's appropriate for the time: after decades of warfare and destruction, the people's enthusiasm helps in the rebuilding of Buddhist temples, which can serve as centers for spreading the teaching.

The Real Buddha Has No Form

On the day when the buddha-images were washed, Daian said:

"The real Buddha has no physical form: what shall we wash? In the garden where Buddha was born, we falsely see an optical illusion. The Zen imperative is carried out, but it has not arrived here today."

The Dawn Sky

At the beginning of the summer retreat, Daian said:

"The ninety-day retreat begins today. I have specially come up to the teaching hall to act as a compass for you.

"One moment unborn, and past, present, and future are cut off: [at that moment,] all the hundred and thousands of buddhas are studying along with you.

"I will not ask what it is that you are studying together. But tell me, right now, where do all the hundreds and thousands of buddhas put their bodies and establish their lives?

"While holding in their hands the talisman that lights up the night, how many know the dawn sky?"

* ───

One moment unborn: A break in the continuity of the false self with its deluded perceptions and judgments allows the wider reality to appear, the reality beyond subjective time and space shared by all the enlightened ones.

The talisman that lights up the night is the meditative concentration that we work to achieve to shed some light into the darkness of our habitual delusion.

The dawn sky stands for the infinite light of the Buddha-Mind that we see encompassing us when the shell of delusion wears through.

Where Will We Meet?

Daian cited a classic Zen story:

"Daowu asked Yunyan, 'After you slough off the leaky shell of physical existence, where will we meet?'

"Yunyan said, 'We will meet where it is neither born nor destroyed.'

"Daowu said, 'Why don't you say we will meet where it is not unborn and undestroyed?'"

Daian commented, "Neither place is right for meeting. If someone asked me where we will see Yunyan after he has sloughed off the leaky shell, I would just say, 'Where won't we meet him?'"

Daian suddenly picked up his staff and drew a line in the air. Then he left the teacher's seat.

* ———————————————————————————

> *Daowu* (768–835) was a student of the great teacher Yaoshan. See cases 55 and 89 in the *Blue Cliff Record.*
>
> *Yunyan* (781–841) studied with the great Zen Teacher Baizhang for twenty years without reaching enlightenment. After Baizhang died, Yunyan went to study with Zen master Yaoshan, and finally awakened. See cases 72 and 89 in the *Blue Cliff Record.*

Abandon It All

Daian said, "Here I have no Buddha Dharma that can be explained and no Zen path that can be studied. You must utterly abandon all that you have had explained to you and all that you have studied at the various Zen centers. Let there be nothing you hold inside you and nothing you depend on outside—then nothing will stop you from being an utterly unconstrained patch-robed monk.

"At just such a time, you must go on to recognize that there is a road of personal transformation."

Daian hit the meditation bench and said, "Red clouds stretch along the blue horizon, the white sun circles the polar mountain."

If You Can Use It

Daian said, "When I opened up the desolate site of the ruined temple here, in the foundations I dug up an axe.

"To the brethren who have been gathered here for a long time I have said: If you can use it, I will give it to you with both hands. If you cannot hold it up, I will take it back."

Suddenly Daian picked up the staff, brandished it once, and said, "The whip is lifted, and the iron ox plows the whole earth. Who can grow fruit trees at the bottom of a well?"

* —————————————————————————————————————

In the foundations I dug up an axe: The axe represents the active wisdom of a bodhisattva.

The iron ox is a symbol for the potential for wisdom and compassion inherent in all of us, which can be stirred into activity (*to plow the whole earth*) by the correct application of Zen methods (*the whip*).

Who can grow fruit trees at the bottom of a well? It is impossible do a bodhisattva's work while still attached to the quietude of solitary meditative absorption.

Lost

Once when a monk asked for instructions, Daian said, "What is lacking in your own portion that you come here to ask for instruction?"

As the monk pondered how to reply, Daian said, "You only know to crave the journey. You are not aware that you have lost your way."

Find Your Own

On the anniversary of Shakyamuni Buddha's enlightenment, Daian cited the traditional story:

"In front of True Awakening Mountain, the World-Honored One saw the morning star, and attained supreme enlightenment.

"He exclaimed, 'How wondrous! All sentient beings are fully endowed with the qualities of the Tathagata's wisdom, but because of the clinging of false thoughts, they cannot realize them.'

"I would like to ask old Shakyamuni what he is calling 'the qualities of wisdom' and what he is calling 'the clinging of false thoughts.' If he hesitated and could not reply, I would hit him across the spine.

"Is there anyone in the assembly who breathes with old Shakyamuni?"

Daian held up his staff and said, "I would not dare expect you to breathe with old Shakyamuni, but it would be good if you could manage to find your own nostrils."

Then Daian leaned on the staff.

Everyone Is Invited

On the morning of New Year's Day, Daian said:

"Before I open my mouth, in all times, in all places, the mind-seal of universal light shows the full brilliance of its pattern.

"If we wait for you to set eyes on it and take a look, you are already confused. This morning I specially point it out to you: I invite everyone to witness the proof."

Vairochana's Seal

Daian asked a monk, "All the worlds in the ten directions are the true seal of Vairochana. Tell me, in whose hands is the handle of the seal?"

The monk hesitated, trying to think what to say. In a severe tone Daian said, "Go away for now and come back another time."

Do You See?

Daian quoted a classic Zen saying: "An ancient worthy said, 'One person is always on the road but has not left home. One person has left home but is not on the road. Tell me, which person should receive the offerings of humans and celestial beings?'"

Daian said, "We won't discuss leaving home or not leaving home, being on the road or not being on the road. I would say: in the whole world, there is only one person, and that one person should receive the offering of humans and celestial beings. Do all of you see that one person?"

He hit the meditation bench and said, "Don't open your eyes! [By the time you deliberately look,] it's long gone."

Climb Up to a Higher Level

Daian said, "When deluded thinking ends, the road of birth-and-death is cut off. When the road of birth-and-death is cut off, the realm of nirvana is empty. Where [in this] do you intend to put the teaching devices of Zen?

"Far, far away in the morning, far, far away in the evening. If you want to get to the depths of the eye that sees a thousand miles, climb up to a higher level."

Buddha's Final Nirvana

On the anniversary of Buddha's death, Daian cited this story:

"At the assembly just before his final nirvana, Buddha rubbed his breast and told the congregation, 'You should observe my body well, with its purple luster and golden hue. Look now until you get your fill, so there will be no regrets later. If you think I am going to become extinct, you are not my disciples. If you think I am not going to become extinct, you are not my disciples.' At that moment, billions of beings in the assembly all achieved enlightenment."

Daian commented, "Buddha's end was a scene of defeat. In the assembly of billions, not one had the energy of a patch-robed monk.

"Do all of you see the World-Honored One rubbing his breast? The water is cold as it flows out of the rock, the wind is fragrant as it passes through the flowers."

* ───────────────────────────────────

In this context, *final nirvana* means Buddha's death.

A Report

Daian held his whisk up vertically and said:

"All the buddhas of the ten directions are on the tip of the whisk, communicating the Dharma-Gate of peaceful living. In the same voice through different mouths they say, 'Ninety days without abandoning the work, a hundred eons are functioning right now.'

"We bump into the barbarian at the crossroads, and he raises his voice and intones, 'How thick is the skin on their faces, that they talk such talk? Let's light a torch and see.' All at once the buddhas and world-honored ones are ashamed and scatter.

"All you monks and followers of Shakyamuni Buddha, how will you breathe along with the buddhas?"

Then Daian hit the meditation bench and said, "In vain do I report an injustice to the guilty parties."

*   ——————————————————————————————

> *Ninety days*: The period of intensive meditation during the annual summer retreat.
>
> *A hundred eons*: The whole karmic legacy that makes up the false self.
>
> *The barbarian at the crossroads*: The embodiment of Zen wisdom, who sees through all provisional teachings, and accepts nothing as sacred.
>
> *Breathe along with the buddhas*: Share in the buddhas' life of wisdom.

You Must Answer

Daian said:

"After the end of the summer retreat, all of you Zen worthies will go off in various directions.

"Suppose that suddenly in a village of three families you bump into a madman who asks you this: 'Eminent one, you have come from Jingshan, so tell me: what did the master who founded the temple there mean when he said, "There are carp on top of the mountains, and there is scattered dust at the bottom of the well"?'

"To succeed, you must answer the madman with skill in means. You cannot quote ancients or moderns to him, or talk of phenomena or inner truth. You cannot shake out your sleeves and go, or spit in his face.

"If you answer him and he doesn't understand, you will earn a rebuke from him, and he will say to you, 'Plenty of fuel and water has been hauled in for you to use on Jingshan, eminent one, but you have never even dreamed of the Buddha Dharma.'

"If you cannot answer him, you also implicate me in your failure.

"This is an iron hammerhead with no hole for the handle."

Daian tapped with the whisk and said, "As all of you travel together on the road down the mountain, your eyes see for themselves the windblown mist."

* ———————————————————————————————————————

Jingshan (Mount Jing), in the vicinity of the great metropolis Hangzhou, was the site of many Buddhist temples.

To earn their keep, Zen monks ought to reach the level of attainment that would enable them to communicate the Dharma to others.

An iron hammerhead with no hole: A dilemma that defeats attempts to rationalize and strikes a blow at the conditioned mind.

Evil Times

Daian said:

"Alas! In the world of evil times in the Age of the End of the Dharma, sentient beings are thin in merit and hard to regulate. We are far from the sages, and perverse views are deeply held. Delusion is strong, the Buddhist teaching is weak, and there are many enemies to do harm. When they hear talk of the sudden teaching of the tathagatas, they regret not being able to wipe it out.

"The formulations of the teaching of enlightenment given by the ancients for one historical period have their proof today, but who is aware of it?

"Nevertheless, let [the enemies of Buddhism] slander it and negate it: lifting a torch to burn the sky, they tire themselves out in vain. When I hear them it is just like drinking sweet dew. They dissolve and melt away and suddenly enter the inconceivable.

"But tell me, whose business is this?" He picked up the staff and hit the incense table and said, "An independently enlightened teacher has come!"

Daian brandished the staff and said, "With superior people, once they decide, they completely comprehend everything. With the middling and lower types, the more they hear, the more they do not believe."

The Age of the End of the Dharma: In the Buddhist view, every particular formulation of the true teaching can only keep its vitality for a finite period of time. Inevitably, the effectiveness of the true teaching is lost, and only a semblance of its forms and traditions remains. Over time, even the semblance decays and crumbles, till nothing is left: this is called the Age of the End of the Dharma. Then the stage is set for a new presentation of the teaching of enlightenment, in the changed circumstances.

Wandering at Play

As the bones of a deceased monk were being interred, Daian said:

"The person who truly travels the Path goes in and out of birth-and-death as if wandering at play.

"But when the sword of doom is hanging over you, how is it? If you cannot think of what to say, your skull falls to the ground."

Where the Tathagata Goes

Daian cited a Zen story:

"Master Zhenjing said, 'In the gate of the patch-robed monks, everything is an infinite world, everything is independent samadhi.'

"Then Zhenjing gave a shout and said, 'Isn't this an infinite world?' Then he coughed and said, 'Isn't this independent samadhi? Ha ha ha! To take this profound mind to serve in the dusty realms of sensory experience is called repaying the benevolence of the buddhas.'"

Then Daian commented, "Revealing infinite worlds and independent samadhi—this is old Zhenjing. In the gate of the patch-robed monks, it still lacks enlightenment. I am not this way."

He picked up the staff and brandished it once and said, "Find it in mind, and everything is unobstructed. Respond to it at hand, and all dharmas are perfected."

Then he leaned on the staff and said, "Others may have their own road through the clouds, but they do not go where the Tathagata goes."

Directly Cutting Through

Daian said, "In the Zen school, we value directly cutting through [false consciousness].

"When asked 'What is Buddha?' Zhaozhou answered, 'The one in the shrine.' When asked 'What is the Path?' Zhaozhou answered, 'The one outside the wall.'

"These are examples of Zen master Zhaozhou cutting directly through for people. Still, I want all of you people to know by directly cutting through."

Then he gave a shout and left the seat.

* ———————————————————————————

> To benefit from Zhaozhou's answers, we must pass beyond the sur-
> face meaning—perhaps starting by asking what shrine? what wall?

An Invitation

Daian said, "The whole earth is a treasury of light. The whole earth is a gate of liberation. The whole earth is a diamond seat. The whole earth is the true body of Vairochana.

"All you people know with the same mind, see with the same eye. Why can't you tell sacred from profane? Why don't you get the independent use of the Buddha-Mind?

"Here today at Jingshan I throw it down in front of you. I invite all of you to witness the proof."

Great Peace

On the morning of New Year's Day, Daian said:

"At the start of the new year, I cannot give you trailing vines. Let us put aside Deshan's blows and Linji's shouts. Master Zhaozhou said that he could use the twenty-four hours of the day, rather than being used by them. You tell me, is there any way to test for this or not?"

Then Daian struck a blow with the whisk and said, "Sun and moon are bright in front of every family's gate. In a time of great peace, there is no use for the fearsome power of a general."

* ───────────────────────────────────

Trailing vines: Verbal explanations, strings of concepts.

Sun and moon: Reality itself, the Buddha-Mind.

In a time of great peace, there is no use for the fearsome power of a general: When the practitioner solidifies the direct perception that reveals the unity of absolute and relative (*in a time of great peace*) there is no further need to struggle (with *the fearsome power of a general*) against entanglement in the sensory world.

The Heroic March

At the end of the summer retreat Daian said:

"The sutra says: 'All phenomena originally of themselves always possess the characteristics of nirvana, but if it were not for all the buddhas who uphold the *Shurangama samadhi*, sentient beings would submit to the karmic consciousness of ignorance.'

"So delusion and enlightenment are in people, not in the Dharma, not in reality itself. The whole summer I have gone in and out with all of you people, but in essence we have never left one-form samadhi. Today is the day we take it easy and do as we please."

Then he held up the staff and said, "It has pierced the nostrils of old Shakyamuni—why don't any of you feel the pain?"

He leaned on the staff and said, "If no mountains block the great ocean, the light of the sky joins directly with the water."

* ────────────────────────────────

> *Shurangama samadhi*, the "heroic march samadhi," refers to the sum total of all the mystic states and stations on the Path, along with all the teaching displays generated by all the enlightened ones in all worlds in all times. If not for these, sentient beings would remain unaware of the absolute reality (*the characteristics of nirvana*) inherent in all relative phenomena.

> *If no mountains block the ocean*: If the false self is not there to block direct perception, one sees the interpenetration of absolute and relative.

Free to Stay or Go

Daian said:

"When the cloth bag of ignorance is opened, the worlds of the ten directions extend in a limitless expanse. Patch-robed monks in straw sandals with staffs across their backs travel in all directions, free to stay or go, irrepressibly happy.

"If suddenly they bump into a phony inspector who asks them, 'What is this business of traveling on foot?' they must answer him well."

Suddenly Daian picked up the staff and brandished it and said,

"If he hadn't shot the tyrant Shi Hu at Indigo Field, who would have known it was the hero General Li?"

Once outside of the bag of ignorance, people are free to stay or go because nothing in the world can entangle them.

* ──────────────────────────────────

The business of traveling on foot is Zen study.

In Daian's time Zen monks were forbidden by law from following the age-old custom of traveling in search of teachers. After two generations of political unrest inspired by folk Buddhist beliefs in the coming of Maitreya, the newly established Ming regime feared the subversive potential of monks freely mingling with the people.

If he hadn't shot the tyrant: How can we know if supposed Zen people are genuine if they have not actually vanquished worldly motivations?

Eloquence

At the cremation of an administrator-monk, Daian said:

"Even if your eloquence pours forth like the Milky Way, and your prose is stitched together of pearls and agate, on the shore of birth-and-death it is totally useless.

"The whole great canon of scriptural teachings is the word 'It.' The Zen patriarch's coming from the west is a footnote."

Daian held up the torch to light the pyre and said, "If you can learn to penetrate through at the gate of intense heat, you will see the Fire God there chanting a mantra."

Autumn

Daian said, "Where is it warm in November? The cassia on the cliff-side wafts its perfume to fill the lonely void. The scenery is cool and pure. The sound of the brook is a dark murmur. The intent of the ancestral teachers is clear—who discerns it?

"The greater and lesser canons of scripture speak of it in every possible way, but it does not go beyond this moment of time. It's the same and not the same, different and not different. How sad, how funny! Old Hanshan has just this moment said, 'My heart is like the autumn moon.'"

Then Daian slapped the meditation bench and left.

* ————————————————————————————————

The same and not the same, different and not different: The intent of the enlightened teachers—their reality and the message they bring of it—is both fused with the ordinary world, yet in a sense also apart from it, a different realm.

Hanshan was a Zen teacher and renowned poet who lived some five hundred years before Daian.

Calling to You

Daian said, "Our school has no words or phrases, nor is there any set doctrine or routine method to give to people. The great teacher Bodhidharma came from south India to our land of China. He transmitted nothing but the mind-seal, to receive people of the supreme vehicle.

"How laughable he was! We should laugh at him for thirty years. If suddenly someone were to come forth from the assembly and say that when I talk this way, I too should be laughed at for thirty years, I would get down off the Zen bench, take him by the hand, and laugh along with him.

"At such a time, there are no buddhas, no patriarchs, no Zen, no Tao, no people, no self. How could we not be happy?"

He held up the staff and said, "Is there anyone here who can do this? Is there?"

He brandished the staff and said, "I'm calling you, my little thieves, I'm waving to you, I'm seeing you off. Don't be surprised by empty explanations. I hope you will take care of yourselves."

Medicine

Daian said, "The sickness is the previous moment of thought deluded. The medicine is the succeeding moment of thought awakened.

"You must make your whole body flow like the wind, and wholly remove medicine and disease. Thus it is said, 'The whole great canon of scriptural teachings are all just prescriptions to cure madmen: they have no real meaning at all.'"

Family Style

Daian cited this case: "A monk asked Yunmen, 'What is your family style, master?' Yunmen answered, 'The people reading books outside the gate will report.'"

Daian spoke a verse in praise:

When you ask the master's family style,
As soon as you open your mouth, it becomes the fall of
   words.
When the people reading books outside the gate come,
Inevitably there will be petty word games.

---
*

The people reading books outside the gate will report: Superficial observers will concoct their own image of Yunmen, and disseminate it among outsiders who know nothing of his reality.

Do Not Quote This Wrongly

Daian said:

"In Zen centers everywhere, they speak of Zen and the Tao and quote ancient and modern. Dragons and elephants crowd around and the Dharma assemblies are flourishing and full.

"Here at Jingshan with one-flavor Zen I settle cases on the basis of the facts. If someone comes in with his whole body covered with silk brocade, I make him go away stark naked. If someone comes in stark naked, I cover his whole body with silk brocade.

"If suddenly there were someone in the assembly to come forth and say, 'How about when they come in neither of these ways?' I would give him twenty blows, and not omit even one. But tell me, everyone, are these blows to reward him or to punish him?"

Then Daian picked up the staff and said, "Later on when you meet people, do not quote this wrongly."

Then he brandished the staff and left the teacher's seat.

Universal Response

At a small gathering on the evening he entered the temple at Yunju, Daian said:

"The spirit light undimmed—for ten thousand ages its message has shown bright. The mirror of wisdom is clear all the way through—it responds universally to everything in space.

"Thus, the Dharma is carried out according to the Dharma, and the Dharma banner is set up according to the place. Sometimes at the crossroads we scatter sand and dirt. Sometimes in the shadow of the thousand peaks we whistle at the moon and wear clouds across our shoulders. It is up to us whether we roll up or roll out, and we release or capture according to the situation.

"The Dharma is like a great bell hanging in an arch. Strike it hard and the sound is great, strike it lightly and the sound is slight. It is like a clear mirror on its stand—when a foreigner comes up to it, a foreigner appears in it, and when a native comes up to it, a native appears in it.

"In the Dharma there is no distinction at all between ancient and modern, nor are there any signs of going or coming. If we hold fast, heaven and earth lose their color. If we let go, pebbles and rubble emit light. At just such a time, tell me, is it right to hold fast or to let go?"

After a silence, Daian said, "When the dragon's sleeves are shaken open, the whole body shows. Where the elephant king walks, there are no fox tracks."

He also spoke a verse:

> I am originally a man from Jiang-Hu who lost his soul.
> For years now, wherever I am, I put the whole body.
> Karmic winds have blown me to Yunju Temple.
> I have won a spirit of peace and joy to rely on.

* ————————————————————————————————

Rolling up or *holding fast*, we keep our focus on the absolute oneness, and the relative world pales. *Rolling out* or *letting go*, we perceive the absolute pervading the relative world, illuminating it, so that *pebbles and rubble emit light.*

Temples of Perfect Enlightenment

Daian said, "If you want to be in harmony right now with the fundamental ground, you simply must abandon all that has gone before. Don't impose conditioned 'knowing' and 'understanding.' Set an eye on before the Buddha was born and take a look: what is it? Suddenly you hit against the void and smash through it. Then you see that all the worlds in the ten directions are all temples of perfect enlightenment. Where else are the mountains, rivers, and the great earth?"

The Man in the Scene

At a small gathering on New Year's Eve at Yunju Temple, a monk asked Daian, "What is the scene at Yunju?"

Daian said, "The road turns, the mountain streams wind around, the empty studio is quiet."

The monk asked, "What is the man in the scene?"

Daian said, "In a time of great peace, a free body."

The monk continued, "Master, we have already received your teachings on the man and the scene. We hope to hear a phrase to receive those with the mentality of beginners."

Daian said, "The hawk without feathers flies stuck to the sky."

Accomplishment

At a small gathering at the end of the summer retreat, Daian said:

"Zen worthies, time passes easily, but it is hard to encounter the teaching of enlightenment.

"As soon as you see the blazing heat of summer, you also see the autumn wind stirring. The ancients established this three-month period for the summer retreat for you to get realization. Try to ponder it carefully and see: in this period of ninety days, what have you accomplished?

"The sutra speaks of 'riding the bodhisattva vehicle, cultivating the practices of nirvana.' But how can you ride the bodhisattva vehicle? How can you cultivate the practices of nirvana?

"If in a moment of thought you can realize your error, then the whole body appears: all vexations are ultimately pure, and the ocean of wisdom of the realm of reality shines through all temporal characteristics like empty space.

"If you cannot do this, you must at least avoid using the thinking mind to try to assess the realm of the perfect enlightenment of the tathagatas."

Open Your Own Eyes

At a small evening gathering Daian said:

"The expedient means of the buddhas and ancestral teachers are as numerous as the river sands. When we check them out, they are all excess verbiage.

"Even if you set out devices in your courtyard and your eloquence flows freely in all directions, if you have not gone beyond the conceptual faculty, you have cheated and lied to yourself in vain.

"If you definitely want to investigate and understand clearly the one transcendent move of the thousand sages, you simply must cut off sensory entanglements and open your own eyes.

"It is present everywhere, clear in everything: the eternal light spontaneously shining, towering up like a wall miles high. All the worlds of the ten directions are the wondrous mind of nirvana. It is impossible to find anything else with the marks of birth and destruction, not even so much as a single atom of dust.

"Eminent monks, do you have a thorough mastery of this? On top of a hundred-foot pole laughing, we transform the body. Then we come back to the meditation hall to sit in the lotus position."

* ———————————————————————————————

Even if you set out devices in your courtyard: Even if you can spin out ideas and images freely.

Impossible to find anything else with the marks of birth and destruction: From the point of view of enlightenment, all impermanent things are like passing reflections in the mirror of the one reality, and the relative is engulfed in the absolute.

Not Much Time

At a small gathering on New Year's Eve, Daian also spoke a verse:

> The evanescent world—not much time.
> Look, look! Another year has passed.
> At our night-time gathering we wish to speak of everlasting
>   things, infinite things.
> What can be done about this madman's lofty stubbornness?

Do You Find Accord?

At a small gathering at the end of the summer retreat, Daian said:

"An ancient said, 'The green, green bamboo is all true Thusness. The thick lush yellow flowers are all transcendent wisdom.'

"Before the Empty Eon, when there were no buddhas or sentient beings, from whom did true Thusness and transcendent wisdom receive their names?

"Here at our Five Topknots Peak, there is an ancient temple a thousand years old. Zen companions come from all around, joining together to dwell in peace.

"Today the ninety days of the summer retreat are complete. I will not ask you about the business of before the Empty Eon. But in your daily activities, do you find accord with your true selves or not?"

After a long silence, Daian said, "Just now there was someone who drew feet on a snake and rolled on into the cave of trailing vines."

He held up the staff and said, "For now, listen to the news the staff has come to reveal."

He planted the staff upright and said, "Let go, as if you have nothing. Of vain efforts and painful sufferings there are a thousand kinds."

He added a verse:

> On a remote mountain top it gets cool—the night air is pure.
> Three months' work is fulfilled—no sentiments remain.
> We want to sell our summer robes, but we stop.
> Seated securely on the meditation cushion, we delight in
>   great peace.

* ───

Just now there was someone who drew feet on a snake and rolled on into the cave of trailing vines: Daian chides his listeners as he sees that they are busy trying to figure out if they are in accord with their true selves.

No Clingings, No Self

At the end of the summer retreat, Daian said:

"Above, no clingings, no looking up in expectation. Below, no sense of personal existence, no self. Everywhere revealing the true workings, in everything fully displaying the wondrous function.

"When we press upon it, the imprint of the ocean of the absolute reality emits light. As soon as you arouse your mind, sensory afflictions have already arisen.

"Just put a stop to all external entanglements, and inwardly your mind will not be so frantic. When your mind is like a wall, then finally you can enter upon the Path.

"The ninety days of summer are over. You are free to go or stay. My duties as abbot are many—no more idle chatter."

Daian struck a blow with the whisk and said, "Those who recognize the benevolence of the buddhas are few, those who spurn the benevolence are many."

*

The imprint of the ocean of the absolute reality: Absolute reality is compared to an ocean, in which all phenomena are like waves. All of our lives, all our moments of consciousness, are like waves in this infinite ocean.

This Dharma-Seal

At a small gathering on New Year's Eve, Daian said:

"This Dharma-Seal of ours: in heaven it's the same as heaven, on earth it's the same as earth. Say ordinary, and it's totally ordinary. Mention holy, and it's totally holy. From ancient times to the present, whether hidden or revealed, there has never been a single phenomenon that was not within it.

"Therefore, when you find it in mind, myriad changes and transformations; when you lose it in intent, myriad differences and discrepancies. All through the year, from beginning to end, it fills your eyes for you to look at, but it seems that you haven't seen it. It fills your ears for you to listen, but it seems you haven't heard it. How is this any different from willingly starving while seated in a platter of food, or willingly dying of thirst while immersed in water?"

Beyond Measure

Daian said, "Great function appears before us, not keeping to set rules. If you yourself are not a person beyond measure, it's impossible for you to understand the affair of communicating enlightenment, which is beyond measure.

"We gather together boundless lands into a single pore, and in that pore build a temple. We compress infinite ages into one moment: is it holy or is it ordinary?

"We invite you all to pause in your travels and dwell peacefully in the wisdom of the inherent equality of all phenomena. Frogs and worms all experience perfect penetration. Manjushri and Samantabhadra are there with them offering congratulations.

"This is the pattern of reality, these are words that accord with inherent nature. If you are devotees of the study of verbal meanings, your vision does not go beyond form and your hearing does not go beyond sound. You distinguish this and that, and talk of defiled and pure, and think that we patch-robed monks are telling empty lies. How can we be surprised at this?"

Then Daian drew a stroke with the staff and said, "When sentiments and sensory experience are totally dissolved away, vision is true—without traversing countless eons, you get the buddhas' body of reality."

* ───────────────────────────────────────

Great function: Enlightened wisdom active in the world.

The Fruit of the Path

Daian said, "The fruit of the path of enlightenment is of itself fundamentally perfectly formed. It does not depend on cultivation or action. How could it be gotten from other people? When sentiments of ordinary and holy end, the essential body shows, true and eternal, clear everywhere, inherent in everything.

"If you reach total comprehension like this, your vision penetrates the root-source. You smash the locked gate of birth-and-death, and overturn the nest of affirmation and denial. All the worlds of the ten directions as a whole are the temple of perfect enlightenment. You wander at play according to circumstances through buddha-lands and palaces of delusion. In brothels and wine shops you dwell in peace, trusting to inherent nature, without any distinction between defiled and pure, without any difference between coming and going.

"This is called the ocean of correct all-embracing knowledge. It is also called the gate of great liberation."

Stainless Study

At a small gathering at the beginning of the summer retreat, Daian said:

"In front of the hall of the ancient buddhas, there has never been any other road. In the gate of the ancestral teachers, how could there be many kinds of talk?

"The Buddha Dharma is not different from the human mind: all inherent functioning is the intent of the enlightened ancestors. The deviation comes because of grasping and false views.

"If you can directly take it up, then you can receive the use of it according to the occasion, far beyond sense-faculties and sense-objects, with objective scenes and subjective knowledge fused together. Whether it is this side or That Side, only you yourself know. You do not have to ask anyone else if it is truth or a semblance of truth, true Dharma or semblance Dharma.

"But if you discriminate among names and forms and go charging forward with interpretive understanding, and think this is adequate for the fundamental study, this is no different from steaming sand to make food.

"Surely you have read this:

"At the Shurangama Assembly the World-Honored One Shakyamuni said to Ananda, 'Even if you go for eons augmenting your learning, it is not as good as one day of stainless study.'

"But tell me, how do you cultivate 'stainless study'? If you say it has cultivation and realization, this is a vulgar lie. If you say it has no cultivation or realization, you are befuddled about buddha-nature.

"Zen worthies, when you get here, to succeed you must investigate with your whole being according to reality, and find someone else who is already enlightened to sort you out.

"Tomorrow we begin our period of intensive practice during the summer retreat, and set a date to get realization. For these ninety days, don't take it easy. Time does not wait for people. Each of us must work hard."

Then Daian struck a blow with his whisk.

*　————————————————————————————

This side and That Side: The realm of ordinary dualistic, subject-object experience, and the realm of enlightened direct perception.

The Shurangama Assembly: Where Shakyamuni Buddha set forth the *Shurangama Sutra*, the *Heroic March Sutra*.

The Zen Wind

When he read the recorded sayings of Master Gulin, Daian composed this verse:

Thirty years and more, he stirred the wind of the Zen
    patriarchs.
The gate of this hermitage does not thunder the same.
The eye for testing people was above his eyebrows.
The device for felling tigers was hidden in the palm of his
    hand.
The dead tree puts out shoots that hang down green to the
    ground.
The cold ashes generate a flame that tinges the sky with red.
Look—he splits open the phrase of undifferentiated
    wholeness.
And wipes away Yangqi's thicket of thorns.

*

The dead tree and *the cold ashes* represent the basis of detachment and dispassion from which the compassion of the Zen teacher operates with expedient means, *putting out shoots* to help enlighten others.

Yangqi was the eleventh-century founder of the line of Zen teachers to which both Gulin and Daian himself belonged.

Looking to the Wind

Daian composed this verse to see off a monk on his travels:

Seeking a teacher, choosing spiritual friends, in order to
  study Zen
Body and mind must be solid as a rock.
A thousand miles looking to the wind, putting an end to
  vainly doing wrong.
One morning speechless, beginning to be happy.
The snow has melted on Yuling Range and the spring travels
  begin.
The moon is full over Fenjiang River as we embark by night.
As we take hold of the black dragon's pearl, the light is
  sparkling bright.
At the summit of the peak where clouds gather, waves flood
  to the sky.

*

Looking to the wind: Exposing oneself to the transformative influence of the Dharma.

The black dragon's pearl: A symbol of enlightenment, which is compared to the legendary precious pearl hidden at the bottom of the sea, guarded by a black dragon.

A Verse of Encouragement

The intimate meaning, the secret meaning, is entirely
    with you—
I have no secret meaning to communicate to people.
If you want to be a seed of light in a time of decline,
Do not study the quietism of other sects.
Suddenly stripped of grasping and rejecting, outside the
    contents of conditioned mind,
Penetrating directly through the treasury of practice before
    the Empty Eon.
When you go into town and extend a hand to people it must
    be done with skill in means.
The Last Age of the Dharma is now in its ten thousandth year.

When Potentials Align

On That Side of your skull there's a spirit light.
It's perfectly clear and unconcealed in daily action.
The Path has no verbal explanations: you must have your
    own insight.
When potentials align, and the mother hen pecks from outside
    the shell while the chick pecks from within,
They must match each other.
Throughout the country the Zen community now is just a
    desolate ruin.
Who can straighten out the decrepit system with his bare hands?

* ───

> *The mother hen and the chick*: A metaphor for the coordinated efforts
> of the enlightened teacher and the student to break through the
> shell of delusion that encloses the student.

Iron Nails

Here on Jingshan I meet the transition from one year to the next
    and celebrate it along with others.
As the family party begins, I do not join the group or feel
    gregarious.
I stir the stew as it cooks, and the fragrance fills the whole place.
Iron nails: the air of food and drink.

* ───────────────────────────────

> *Iron nails* are used as a metaphor for the bonds of conviviality
> because the social process of consensual validation can rivet people
> to conventional reality.

A Gate of Awakening

(A verse in reply to the disciple of a Dharma-brother:)

Before the Buddha was born, the One Matter of
    Enlightenment:
So cheap it can be denigrated, so dear it can be honored.
Only when there's nowhere to seek on the verbal route
Do we finally know for sure that Zen has a gate of awakening.
A snap of the fingers, and past, present, and future are
    cut off.
In the end, we are not confused by the six sense-objects.
If not for the visit of my Dharma-nephew,
How would I open my old mouth to discuss it?

What Can Stop You?

The treasury of practices is not apart from the Path.

Preserve it well twenty-four hours a day.

As you suddenly put a stop to the myriad entanglements, there is
  no other road.

As soon as you arouse a single thought, there are many divergent paths.

How can it be sought from anyone else?

What can stop you from getting your own knowledge of the ultimate understanding?

In the treasury, the light of the wish-granting jewel is shining
  bright:

Pick it up and it melts away everyone's doubts.

* ———————————————————————————

> *The wish-granting jewel* symbolizes the direct perception inherent in
> our buddha-nature.

Gazing Like a Wall

In an empty house, gazing like a wall

Speaking or silent, never setting foot in the city streets

Just bringing up the seal of the patriarchs before my own mental
  impulses start working

Following the secret spirit talisman the Zen patriarchs wore

In the mirror, my beard, a thousand snow-white strands

At the corner of the bench, a rattan cane, seven feet of black

My only fear is that a summons will arrive from on high

With an imperial grant of a golden robe to chase me to court

It Cannot Be Concealed

Everywhere seeking teachers and spiritual friends to study with.

Splitting apart the mass of doubt, unfurling the light of wisdom,

One phrase that matches the potential transmits the Dharma-
   Seal.

Ten years mixing your tracks in the Zen halls.

The cold pine rears up its trunk, its top in the frigid clouds.

The autumn chrysanthemums stretch forth their flowers in a
   band of dewy yellow.

Wondrous function appears in full everywhere.

Completely understand the secret treasury: it cannot be
   concealed.

Riding the Ox Backward

The ox comes pure: we don't apply the whip.

The flat plain is boundless, the grass grows lush.

At ease, sitting astride him backward, riding out the gate.

A single note from the horizontal flute, so high it pierces heaven.

* ──────────────────────────────

The ox represents the Buddha-Mind. Carried along by the power of the Buddha-Mind, facing *backward* into the realm of conventional reality, the enlightened ones *ride out the gate* to do the work of bodhisattvas.

The flat plain represents the phenomenal world as it appears to the Equality Wisdom of the enlightened: *the grass grows lush* when the inherent equality of all things is realized, so that the phenomenal world becomes an arena of enlightened action.

A single note from the flute represents the expression of the enlightening teaching.

Expounding the Dharma Together

Before you even wet your writing brush with ink, your
    literary brilliance shows.
As soon as I open my mouth, my tongue goes dead.
Last night empty space was laughing aloud:
The dense array of myriad images were all expounding
    the Dharma together.

The Garden of Knowledge

The garden of knowledge seems deep as the ocean.
It's better to travel and search with a light satchel and
    a short walking stick.
A thousand roads circling a thousand mountains.
One inch of time, one inch of gold.

* ───────────────────────────────────

> *One inch of time, one inch of gold*: For a person traveling the Bud-
> dhist path, every moment is precious.

Melting Down a Bell

In the blast furnace is where the body is transformed.
When it opens its mouth, it must know there is someone who will
    appreciate the sound.
How many monks line up and listen
To hear its commands thunder through the forest?

* ───────────────────────────────────

> *In the blast furnace*: A metaphor for Zen practice.

Beyond

Pouring down, the "plum rain" materializing out of the mists
  splashes on the upper story.
As I sit alone in solitary silence, myriad concerns are purified out.
The grass is deep on the path in front of my gate: human foot-
  prints are few.
At ease on the meditation bench: a stick of rattan to whip myself
  with if I slack off.
July, but the mountain hut is cold as ice.
In the red dusts of the city streets the noise is rumbling and
  surging.
Notions of profit and fame and conditioned mind and conscious-
  ness have all dissolved away and ended:
A monk beyond things, thoroughly pure and at ease.

Do not say that heaven and earth go against great certainty.
Spontaneous fit without partiality all follows accordingly.
The blue seas and the mulberry fields change of themselves;
Nothing departs from the seal of the mind-ground.
Before you are clear about the mind-ground, it is all scalding
  steam;
When you manage to illuminate it clearly, as before it seems
  as if you never have.
Take care, all you traveling patriarchs who go everywhere
  to study,
So that in the future you all will be able to perpetuate the
  True Lamp.

* ———————————————————————————————

  Spontaneous fit without partiality: This describes the actions of an
  enlightened person who meets the needs of situations without personal biases or preferences getting in the way.

The Family Jewels

The precious treasury is thrown open: what is there?
In all places it's our own family jewels.
From the ancestral teachers we have personally received the
   matching half of the ticket.
We should bring it out as much as we can to benefit and help
   people.

Invoking Buddha

Invoking Buddha is nothing but invoking inherent mind.
Your own inherent mind is buddha: don't seek elsewhere.
Right before our eyes, even the forest trees and ponds
Express the sound of the Dharma day and night.

* ———————————————————————————

> *Invoking Buddha* refers to the Pure Land Buddhist practice of recit-
> ing the name of Amitabha Buddha. Amitabha was a buddha of the
> remote past who vowed to come to the aid of anyone who invoked
> his name. According to the Pure Land teaching, people can achieve
> rebirth in a Pure Land free of suffering, sickness, and death by rely-
> ing on the power of Amitabha Buddha and invoking his name with
> single-minded focus.
>
> In the Zen interpretation of Pure Land practice, reciting the buddha-
> name is a means of achieving mindfulness of the inherent Buddha-
> Mind by interrupting conditioned consciousness.
>
> *Even the forest trees and ponds express the sound of the Dharma day
> and night:* According to the Pure Land teaching, the very landscape
> of Amitabha's Pure Land constantly teaches the Dharma. In the Zen
> view, even the physical features of the present world express reality,
> because the phenomenal world is just a manifestation of the
> absolute Buddha-Mind.

The Natural Real Buddha

(A verse to a Buddhist layman:)

> The true self in every person is the natural real buddha.
> Through every hour of the day and night it is always emitting
>   light.
> If you can manage to see it personally as you lift your
>   eyebrows,
> Why bother making special trips all over to pay your respects
>   to Zen masters?

Stuck Inside Their Shells

The episode of expounding the Dharma in the Tushita Palace—
Blue sky, white sun, rumbling gales and thunder.
So many people stuck in their shells, sealed within delusion—
They discuss the Buddha Dharma as a special marvel, while
    their faces are covered with dust.

* ——

> The story goes that on one occasion when Shakyamuni Buddha was
> living in a palace in the Tushita Heaven, prior to his earthly incar-
> nation, he emitted light from beneath his feet that shone on all the
> worlds of the ten directions. When the light reached hell, all the
> beings there who had previously planted the seeds of goodness were
> touched by the light; this enabled them to escape from hell and be
> reborn in Tushita Heaven.

To Friends in the Path

If you want to investigate the transcendent devices of the Zen
    house,

Put on the armor of energetic progress, arouse its full awesome
    power,
And with the sword of wisdom, cut to pieces the net of ignorance.
I guarantee that with mind empty, you will return home
    successful.

To a Woman of the Path

In the world of the five corruptions, it is impossible to abide for
    long.
How many times has the boundless ocean of the eons dried up?
If you empty out past, present, and future with one moment
    equanimous and at ease,
Then you can be called a real woman of power.

* ───────────────────────────────

The world of the five corruptions: A concept from Buddhist cosmology, that as an era proceeds through time, it is more and more
afflicted with corruption: the corruption of the era, the corruption of
views, the corruption of afflictions, the corruption of living beings,
the corruption of life itself.

The Golden Lock

(A verse to see off his attendant:)

The attendant has finished his study of Zen.
Last night empty space laughed out loud.
Each and every person inherently possesses the treasury
    of light:
It takes the jade key to open the golden lock.

* ───────────────────────────────

The jade key of wisdom opens *the golden lock* of perception and
reveals Buddha-Mind, *the treasury of light.*

Ten Verses on Dwelling in the Mountains

Living on a remote peak, worldly thoughts forgotten,
There's no more Buddha Dharma to discuss.
I only rise from my slumber when the sun is high.
On the trellis the roses are just now fragrant.

The roots of the pine sit in a gnarled mass upon the rocks.
A piece of idle cloud goes and comes.
Few are the sharp-spirited monks who pass by.
The gate of rough wood stands open all day long: for whom?

Cloudy mountains fill the eye, the stillness of spring.
Without words, the peach is ever so sweet in the sunlight.
Straightaway, myriad impulses all cease.
For this Path, why bother pointing out the direction any more?

The road here twists and turns and doubles back, overgrown
    with grass waist-high.
A few thatched huts beside the mountain summit.
Only the moon in the sky knows my heart.
How many times has it flown by, keeping me company
    in my silent solitude?

Smoke from the fragrant incense melts away as I wake up
    from a noontime nap.
Distant mountains come into view in layers of jade green.
There are no constraints in this pure and peaceful world.
A long line of gruel-eating monks.

Body covered with hair, a robe of cotton patches,
I shake off the blue-black ashes, which fly up in
    the window.

In front of the gate a little dog is yapping,
Happy to see the mountain lad returning with a load of rice.

On the empty stairs after the rain, pacing back and forth alone,
Autumn hues greenish and cool, the sun's shadow low.
The sound of the woodcutters' song comes to the valley mouth.
The bamboo-bird flies up to the treetops to give its call.

In the world, my heart was like January ice.
Dwelling in the mountains, I laugh to myself at my total
   incompetence.
Don't use up the oil cooking the vegetable stew.
Leave a bit to offer in the buddha-lamp in front of the hall.

The stone room is deserted as I sit among the greenery.
It's rare for old friends from Jiang-Hu to come.
In the assemblies of the Southeast there are many elephants and
   dragons.
Do you know which ones are truly extolling the workings of the
   ancestral teachers?

Living at ease according to my lot, passing the years,
Working to uphold the clan of my forebears, embarrassed to
   leave home.
Night after night the north wind rises, scouring the earth.
Again I see the color of spring arriving on the plum blossoms.

A Living Eye

When you see the Tao, you can cultivate the Tao.
When you recognize benevolence, you should repay benevolence.
Great accomplishments do not start with imposing control.

The subtle cut leaves no mark.

Every land is a treasury of magical powers.

Every atom of dust is a gate of wisdom shining.

Open a living eye prior to any mental impulses:

One phrase settles heaven and earth.

Buddhism for Householders

To be able to learn Buddhism while living at home,

You must vow to keep the vegetarian diet and the precepts
   your whole life long.

If you want to experience the fruit of uncontrived action,

You must eliminate the causal bases of defilement,

Then, with wondrous function everywhere whole,

Meshing with natural reality in every particular,

Though you live in the world of sensory affliction,

You are fit to be called a liberated person.

True Gold

(To a woman of the Path:)

The Great Path has no location:

It appears everywhere in everything.

As soon as false sentiments cease,

Enlightened nature is perfectly clear of itself.

The ancient mirror is polished again and again till it shines.

True gold is refined a hundred times till it's pure.

Please look at daughter Lingzhao:

For a thousand years she has inspired people with her
   fair reputation.

* ───

Lingzhao, her brother, and her father Pang Yun were three Zen adepts who lived as laypeople in ninth-century China. As the family moved around, Lingzhao helped meet expenses by selling the bamboo ware she wove.

One of Layman Pang's verses goes: "I have a son who has not married / I have a daughter I have not married off / The whole family gathers round / And together we talk of birthlessness."

A Grand Presence

(To a layman:)

The naturally real buddha is inherent nature,
A grand presence amid daily activities.
Once you have carefully cultivated your intent for the Tao,
You must advance in your sitting meditation work.
When there are no obstructions wherever you touch,
And you master adaptive change when faced with dynamic
    situations,
With mind empty, you can make the grade:
You must be the same as Old Layman Pang.

Self-Praise

Face cold as iron,
Heart dead as ashes,
No Zen to talk,
A mouth that opens wearily.
Serving before the heavenly palace, I have sat in response
    to the imperial summons.
From the summit of the cool misty peak, I came to court in
    obedience to the imperial will.

Lame and unsteady,

Stupid and dumb,

A blind shavepate who brings disaster to the Zen community,

An old fist that must punch Zen men in the face.

Index

About the Translator

J.C. Cleary is the translator of many Zen works. He has a Ph.D. in East Asian Languages and Civilizations from Harvard University and served an apprenticeship as a translator with Thomas Cleary.

After working as a daycare teacher for many years, and then teaching college, he went into the software industry where he now works as a domain analyst and interface designer.

Previous publications:

The Blue Cliff Record (with Thomas Cleary, Shambhala, 1977)

Swampland Flowers (Grove Press, 1977; reprinted 2005)

Zen Lore from the Source Mirror (Nanyang Books, 1979)

Zen Dawn (Shambhala, 1986)

A Buddha from Korea (Shambhala, 1988)

Zibo (Asian Humanities Press, 1989)

Worldly Wisdom (Shambhala, 1991)

A Tune Beyond the Clouds (Asian Humanities Press, 1991)

Meditating with Koans (Asian Humanities Press, 1992)

Zen Letters (with Thomas Cleary, Shambhala, 1994)

Pure Land Pure Mind (Sutra Translation Committee of the U.S. and Canada, 1994)

The Mind Seal of the Buddhas (Sutra Translation Committee of the U.S. and Canada, 1996)

Recorded Sayings of Linji (Bukkyo Dendo Kyokai, 1998)

Wumen's Barrier (Bukkyo Dendo Kyokai, 1998)

Bequeathed Teaching Sutra (Bukkyo Dendo Kyokai, 2004)

Working Toward Enlightenment (Samuel Weiser, 1993)

Authorship and Translation of the *Great Perfection of Wisdom Treatise* (2004)

The Lotus Sutra (forthcoming)

About Wisdom

Wisdom Publications, a nonprofit publisher, is dedicated to making available authentic works relating to Buddhism for the benefit of all. We publish books by ancient and modern masters in all traditions of Buddhism, translations of important texts, and original scholarship. Additionally, we offer books that explore East-West themes unfolding as traditional Buddhism encounters our modern culture in all its aspects. Our titles are published with the appreciation of Buddhism as a living philosophy, and with the special commitment to preserve and transmit important works from Buddhism's many traditions.

To learn more about Wisdom, or to browse books online, visit our website at www.wisdompubs.org.

You may request a copy of our catalog online or by writing to this address:

Wisdom Publications
199 Elm Street
Somerville, Massachusetts 02144 USA
Telephone: 617-776-7416
Fax: 617-776-7841
Email: info@wisdompubs.org
www.wisdompubs.org

The Wisdom Trust

As a nonprofit publisher, Wisdom is dedicated to the publication of Dharma books for the benefit of all sentient beings and dependent upon the kindness and generosity of sponsors in order to do so. If you would like to make a donation to Wisdom, you may do so through our website or our Somerville office. If you would like to help sponsor the publication of a book, please write or email us at the address above.

Thank you.

Wisdom is a nonprofit, charitable 501(c)(3) organization affiliated with the Foundation for the Preservation of the Mahayana Tradition (FPMT).